D0460232

approaching eye level

vivian gornick

approaching eye level

beacon press boston

Beacon Press
25 Beacon Street, Boston, Massachusetts 02108-2892
http://www.beacon.org

Beacon Press Books are published under the auspices of
the Unitarian Universalist Association of Congregations.

Printed in the United States of America

01 00 99 98   8 7 6 5 4 3

Text design by Anne Chalmers
Composition by Electronic Publishing Services, Inc.

Library of Congress Cataloging-in-Publication data
can be found on page 166.

contents

approaching eye level

1 on the street: nobody watches, everyone performs

A WRITER WHO LIVED AT THE END OF MY block died. I'd known this woman more than twenty years. She admired my work, shared my politics, liked my face when she saw it coming toward her, I could see that, but she didn't want to spend time with me. We'd run into each other on the street, and it was always big smiles, a wide embrace, kisses on both cheeks, a few minutes of happy unguarded jabber. Inevitably I'd say, "Let's get together." She'd nod and say, "Call me." I'd call, and she'd make an excuse to call back, then she never would. Next time we'd run into each other: big smile, great hug, kisses on both cheeks, not a word about the unreturned call. She was impenetrable: I could not pierce the mask of smiling politeness. We went on like this for years. Sometimes I'd run into her in other parts of town. I'd always be startled, she too, New York is like a country, the neighbor-hood is your town, you spot someone from the block or the building in another neighborhood and the first impulse to the brain is, What are *you* doing here? We'd each see the thought on the other's face and start to laugh. Then we'd both give a brief salute and keep walking.

Six months after her death I passed her house one day and felt stricken. I realized that never again would I look at her re-treating back thinking, Why doesn't she want my friendship? I missed her then. I missed her terribly. She was gone from the landscape of marginal encounters. That landscape against which I measure daily the immutable force of all I connect with only on the street, and only when it sees me coming.

At Thirty-eighth Street two men were leaning against a build-ing one afternoon in July. They were both bald, both had cigars in their mouths, and each one had a small dog attached to a leash. In the glare of noise, heat, dust, and confusion, the dogs barked nonstop. Both men looked balefully at their ani-mals. "Yap, yap, stop yapping already," one man said angrily. "Yap, yap, keep on yapping," the other said softly. I burst out laughing. The men looked up at me, and grinned. Satisfaction spread itself across each face. They had performed and I had received. My laughter had given shape to an exchange that would otherwise have evaporated in the chaos. The glare felt less threatening. I realized how often the street achieves com-position for me: the flash of experience I extract again and again from the endless stream of event. The street does for me what I cannot do for myself. On the street nobody watches, everyone performs.

Another afternoon that summer I stood at my kitchen sink struggling to make a faulty spray attachment adhere to the inside of the faucet. Finally, I called in the super in my building. He shook his head. The washer inside the spray was too small for the faucet. Maybe the threads had worn down. I should go to the hardware store and find a washer big enough to remedy the situation. I walked down Greenwich Avenue, carrying the faucet and the attachment, trying hard to remember exactly what the super had told me to ask for. I didn't know the language, I wasn't sure I'd get the words right. Suddenly, I felt anxious, terribly anxious. I would not, I knew, be able to get what I needed. The spray would never work again. I walked into Garber's, an old-fashioned hardware store with these tough old Jewish guys behind the counter. One of them—also bald and with a cigar in his mouth—took the faucet and the spray in his hand. He looked at it. Slowly, he began to shake his head. Obviously, there was no hope. "Lady," he said. "It ain't the threads. It definitely ain't the threads." He continued to shake his head. He wanted there to be no hope as long as possible. "And this," he said, holding the gray plastic washer in his open hand, "this is a piece of crap." I stood there in patient despair. He shifted his cigar from one side of his mouth to the other, then moved away from the counter. I saw him puttering about in a drawerful of little cardboard boxes. He removed something from one of them and returned to the counter with the spray magically attached to the faucet. He detached the spray and showed me what he had done. Where there had once been gray plastic there was now gleaming silver. He screwed the spray back on, easy as you please. "Oh," I crowed, "you've done it!" Torn between the triumph of problem-solving and the satisfaction of denial, his mouth twisted up in a grim smile. "Metal," he said philosophically, tapping the perfectly fitted washer in the faucet. "This," he picked up the plastic again, "this is a piece of crap. I'll take two dollars and fifteen cents from you." I thanked him profusely, handed him his money, then clasped my hands together on the counter and said, "It is such a pleasure to have small anxieties easily corrected." He looked at me. "Now," I said, spreading my arms wide, palms up, as though about to introduce a vaudeville act, "you've freed me for large anxieties." He continued to look at me. Then he shifted his cigar again, and spoke. "What you just said. That's a true thing." I walked out of the store happy. That evening I told the story to Laura, a writer. She said, "These are your people." Later in the evening I told it to Leonard, a New Yorker. He said, "He charged you too much."

Street theater can be achieved in a store, on a bus, in your own apartment. The idiom requires enough actors (bit players as well as principals) to complete the action and the rhythm of extended exchange. The city is rich in both. In the city things can be kept moving until they arrive at point. When they do, I come to rest.

•   •   •

I complain to Leonard of having had to spend the evening at a dinner party listening to the tedious husband of an interesting woman I know.

"The nerve," Leonard replies. "He thinks he's a person too."

Marie calls to tell me Em has chosen this moment when her father is dying to tell her that her self-absorption is endemic not circumstantial.

"What bad timing," I commiserate.

"Bad timing!" Marie cries. "It's aggression, pure aggression!" Her voice sounds the way cracked pavement looks.

Lorenzo, a nervous musician I know, tells me he is buying a new apartment.

"Why?" I ask, knowing his old apartment to be a lovely one.

"The bathroom is twenty feet from the bedroom," he confides, then laughs self-consciously. "I know it's only a small detail. But when you live alone it's all details, isn't it?"

I run into Jane on the street. We speak of a woman we both know whose voice is routinely suicidal. Jane tells me the woman called her the other day at seven ayem and she responded with exuberance. "Don't get me wrong," she says, "I wasn't being altruistic. I was trying to pick her up off the ground because it was too early in the morning to bend over so far. I was just protecting my back."

My acquaintanceship—like the city itself—is wide-ranging but unintegrated. The people who are my friends are not the friends of one another. Sometimes—when I am feeling expansive and imagining life in New York all of a piece—these friendships feel like beads on a necklace loosely strung, the beads not touching one another but all lying, nonetheless, lightly and securely against the base of my throat, magically pressing into me the warmth of connection. Then my life seems to mirror an urban essence I prize: the dense and original quality of life on the margin, the risk and excitement of having to put it all together each day anew. The harshness of the city seems alluring. Ah, the pleasures of conflict! The glamour of uncertainty! Hurrah for neurotic friendships and yea to incivility!

At other times—when no one is around and no one is available—I stare out the window, thinking, What a fool you are to glamorize life in the city. Loneliness engulfs me like dry heat. It is New York loneliness, hot with shame, a loneliness that tells you you're a fool and a loser. Everyone else is feasting, you alone cannot gain a seat at the banquet. I look down at the street. I see that mine is a workhorse life. As long as I remain in harness I am able to put one foot in front of the other without losing step, but if anything unbalances me I feel again the weight of circumstance hanging from my neck, a millstone beneath which I have taught myself to walk upright.

The day is brilliant: asphalt glimmers, people knife through the crowd, buildings look cut out against a rare blue sky. The sidewalk is mobbed, the sound of traffic deafening. I walk slowly, and people hit against me. Within a mile my pace quickens, my eyes relax, my ears clear out. Here and there, a face, a body, a gesture separates itself from the endlessly advancing crowd, attracts my reviving attention. I begin to hear the city, and feel its presence. Two men in their twenties, thin and well dressed, brush past me, one saying rapidly to the other, "You gotta give her credit. She made herself out of nothing. And I mean nothing." I laugh and lose my rhythm. Excuse me, my fault, beg your pardon. . . . A couple appears in the crowd, dark, attractive, middle-aged. As they come abreast of me the man is saying to the woman, "It's always my problem. It's never your problem." Cars honk, trucks screech, lights change. Sidewalk vendors hawk food, clothing, jewelry. A man standing beside a folding table covered with gold and silver watches speaks quietly into the air. "It's a steal, ladies and gentlemen," he says. "A real steal." Another couple is coming toward me, this time an odd one. The woman is black, a dwarf, around forty years old. The man is Hispanic, a boy, twelve or fourteen. She looks straight ahead as she walks, he dances along beside her. As they pass she says in the voice of a Montessori mother, "It doesn't matter what he thinks. It only matters what you think."

My shoulders straighten, my stride lengthens. The misery in my chest begins to dissolve out. The city is opening itself to me. I feel myself enfolded in the embrace of the crowded street, its heedless expressiveness the only invitation I need to not feel shut out.

There are mornings I awake and, somehow, I have more of myself. I swing my legs over the side of the bed, draw up the blind, and, from my sixteenth-floor window, feel the city spilling itself across my eyes, crowding up into the world, filling in the landscape. Behind it, there in the distance, where it belongs, is the Hudson River and, if I want it, the sky. But I don't want it. What I want is to take this self I now have more of down into those noisy, dirty, dangerous streets and make my way from one end of Manhattan to the other in the midst of that crowd that also may have more of itself. There is no friend, lover, or relative I want to be with as much as I want to swing through the streets being jostled and bumped, catching the eye of the stranger, feeling the stranger's touch. In the street I am grinning like an idiot to myself, walking fast at everyone coming my way. Children stare, men smile, women laugh right into my eyes. The tenderness I encounter in that mood! The impersonal affection of a palm laid against my arm or my back as someone murmurs, "Excuse me," and sidles skillfully past my body: it soothes beyond reasonable explanation. I feel such love then, for the idea of the city as well as the reality. And everyone looks good: handsome, stylish, interesting. Life spills over without stint and without condition. I feel often that I am walking with my head tipped back, my mouth thrown open, a stream of sunlight on water pouring into my throat. When I consider the days on which I find myself looking into one gargoyle face after another—everyone in front of me old, ugly, deformed, and diseased—I have to realize the street gives me back a primitive reflection of whatever load of hope or fear I am carrying about with me that day.

Nothing heals me of a sore and angry heart like a walk

through the very city I often feel denying me. To see in the
street the fifty different ways people struggle to remain human until the very last minute—the variety and inventiveness
of survival technique—is to feel the pressure relieved, the
overflow draining off. I join the anxiety. I share the condition.
I feel in my nerve endings the common refusal to go under.
Never am I less alone than alone in the crowded street. Alone,
I imagine myself. Alone, I buy time. Me, and everyone I know.
Me, and all the New York friends.

The telephone rings. It's Leonard with a question about an editor he wants to send someone to. I answer his question, and
we chat. I hear the bright hard edge in his voice, I hear him
struggling against it. I help by talking us into a conversation
that interests us both. In ten minutes he's been pulled out of
his own black hole. He's laughing now, quite genuinely.
Warmed by the effort and the success, I say, "Let's have dinner." "Sure," he responds with only a flicker of hesitation.
"Let's see now." He's looking at his book. "God, this is awful!"
I can hear the anxiety seeping back into his voice, the panic he
feels at being forced to make a date. "How about two weeks
from Friday?" "Fine," I say, only a second or two off course
myself.

Later in the day the phone rings again. It's Laura. "You
won't believe this," she says, and proceeds to entertain us both
with the story she's called to tell me. Laura is all solid contact
from the moment her voice hears mine. She tells the story, we

both laugh, many sentences of psychological wisdom pass between us. "Let's have dinner," I say. "Absolutely," she says. "Let's see now." She too looks at her book. "Omigod, this is ridiculous. I can't do it until early next week. Waitaminnit, waitaminnit." She's enjoying her own self so much during this conversation she doesn't want to let the pleasure evaporate. "There's something here I can change. How about Thursday?"

There are two categories of friendship: those in which people are enlivened by each other and those in which people must be enlivened to be with each other. In the first category one clears the decks to be together. In the second one looks for an empty space in the schedule.

Sometimes I am Laura, sometimes Leonard. Sometimes I am both in the course of a single day. I am eager to remain Laura. She is always responsive to human contact. To be responsive is to feel expressive. I value the expressiveness above all else. Or so I say. But there are moments, even days, when any disinterested observer might justly conclude that I, like Leonard, seem awash in my own melancholy, swamped by the invading instability, suffering a failure of nerve to which I seem devoted.

New York friendship is an education in the struggle between devotion to the melancholy and attraction to the expressive. I had thought it would be different in friendship than it generally is in marriage: attaining to a higher level of equilibrium somehow. But how foolish to have thought that. We are all the formerly married, are we not. Most of us spend our lives fighting an inner battle that is never won, in a war

concluded only by death. In each life, however, one element
or the other has the edge. The city reels beneath the impact
of this dynamic. Why, exactly, it's hard to say.

I put the telephone receiver back in its cradle. I close the
apartment door. In thirty seconds I'm on the street. Thank
God for the street! Those of us who crave the expressive but
can't shake off the melancholy walk the street. The pavements
of New York are filled with people escaping the prison sentence of personal history into the promise of an open destiny.

This morning, on Eighth Avenue in Chelsea, I saw a woman I
thought I knew, a faculty wife I'd once met somewhere in the
South. The woman's face was narrow and fine boned, framed
in a waterfall of New York kinky hair, just like Barbara Levinson's. And she was wearing worn leather boots that had once
been expensive along with a wool cape three years out of fash-
ion held together by a jade and silver clasp, also just the kind
of thing Barbara might have worn. When I got close I saw that
it was not Barbara at all. How knowing this face was! It was the
face of a woman who had had "expectations," you could see
that. The mouth was ravaged, the chin defiant, the lipstick
bold, the eyes resigned to intelligent obscurity. The woman
looked glamorous to me here on Eighth Avenue at ten in the
morning—richly haggard, a jewel in its natural setting—with
the street at her back and all that she knew etched clearly
in her face. It was a face that could have been made only in
the city.

In the South Barbara L. had seemed odd, an embarrassing

exotic, and then as she got older just embarrassing. It was the isolation that had done her in, I could see that now. One among the many, she could survive in the South but not flourish. On the way to interesting she had stopped at eccentric. To blossom just "anywhere" one must be either distinguished enough to create one's own environment or humble enough to merge with the one at hand. If one is neither, a critical mass of like-minded spirits is required. It's like the difference between ordinary plants put down in a suburban lawn (one dumb-looking bush here, a forlorn flowerbed there) and those in a richly planted garden whose massed profusion makes the same homely bushes and flowers glow with "element." Here on Eighth Avenue what this woman knew made her exciting. Put her down in a southern college town and she'd quickly become forlorn.

That hair. That New York kinky hair. It required more massed profusion than any of us had ever dreamed it would.

On Ninth Avenue, near the bus station, suddenly there is a couple walking beside me, in the gutter, among the cars. They are both black, both thin, and both dressed in rags. The man carries a heavy shopping bag in each hand. The woman walks behind the man, carrying nothing, trembling with fatigue. The man seems beyond speech. He moves stoically ahead. She moves slowly with great hesitation. Her face weeps without a sound. She cries out at him, "You no good! You no good at all. You take everything from me. Everything!" The man makes no reply. The woman repeats that he is no good and that he has taken everything from her. "You one no good man," she calls out again. "I gonna call the poh-leece on you. You heah me? I gonna call the poh-leece." To my astonishment she does indeed stop a cop and demand that he attend to her complaint. A crowd begins to gather. The cop hears the woman out. The man with the shopping bags stops walking. I see the effort it costs him to bring his plodding motion to a halt. The cop turns to the man. The man says quietly that he has taken nothing from her, that he is carrying her load as well as his own. The cop nods wearily. He and the man quickly become allies. The cop puts a kindly hand on his arm and one on the woman's arm. He urges them to repair their quarrel and sends them on their way. The woman stands there, helpless, all hope now gone. The man waits, looking patiently at her. He knows he must let her speak. The woman extends her arm, makes a fist of her hand. From the fist she extends her forefinger and shakes it like a thermometer at the man. "I don' want no part of you," she cries out. "You stay away from me! I don' wan' no part of you no more." Slowly, the other fingers of her clenched fist open out. These fingers then begin to curl inward. They open and close in a beckoning motion. "I don' wan' no part of you," she cries. The fingers begin to implore instead of accuse. Swifter and swifter, they beckon. And all the while she keeps on crying, "I don' wan' no part of you."

I stand alone at the edge of the crowd. The woman's voice and gesture thrill me. I am amazed by her eloquence. How well she has put language and movement together to tell her story. I do not feel at one with her. She is alone, I am alone. But there she is, and here I am. She too has New York kinky hair. For the moment that's comradeship enough.

When I was growing up New York was safe, everything was either cheap or free, and, in midtown, no gays, no blacks, no women. Now the city is violent, everything costs the earth, and we are all visible.

In the middle of the intersection at Thirty-fourth and Second two cars have nearly collided. Both are stopped at angles of craziness, doors flung open, each driver out of the car, screaming. Instantly, the crowd gathers. A cop walks over. Both drivers scream at him, "Man, you see what he did? You see what he *did?*" The cop places a hand on the arm of each man and says, "I'm now about to administer justice. You," he nods at one and points east, "get in your car. You," he nods at the other and points west, "get in *your* car. And both of you, get the fuck out of here." The crowd applauds.

On the corner of Twenty-third and Seventh a man with a navy blue wool cap jammed onto his head, shivering inside a fake leather jacket, stands selling an old *Daily News* for a quarter, on his face a sinister smile. The headline reads: SADDAM SHOT. The man calls out softly, "Read all about it. Read all about it. They're shooting at your friend and mine. Send him your love, send him a card, send him a bomb. Let him *know* how you feel." Closure at last on America in the Persian Gulf.

In front of the Coliseum a hawker stands selling some gadget that everyone is passing up. "One dolla, one dolla, only a dolla, folks," he drones. "Get it while you can. Just today, one dolla, one dolla." Only his mouth is moving, his face is silent, his eyes dead. A young woman passes in the crowd. She works in the neighborhood. The hawker knows her. "One dolla, only a dolla. . .Nice ta see ya, darlin, *nice* ta see ya, how are ya taday. . .A dolla, folks, only a dolla." It's shocking to hear his voice break the drone, quicken into life, resume the drone. Her cheeks color up. She doesn't mind. She nods in recognition. "Good," she says in a low tone and keeps moving. The expression on each face intensifies: on his pleasure, on hers relief. Clearly, its a ritual. Thirty seconds a day these two rescue each other deep in the middle of the anonymous crowd.

The street keeps moving, and you've got to love the movement. You've got to find the composition of the rhythm, lift the story from the motion, understand and not regret that all is dependent on the swiftness with which we come into view and pass out again. The pleasure and the reassurance lie precisely in the speed with which connection is established and then let go of. No need to clutch. The connection is generic not specific. There's another piece of it coming right along behind this one.

On the Sixth Avenue bus I get up to give an old woman my seat. She's small and blond, wearing gold jewelry and a mink coat, her hands a pair of blotchy claws with long red fingernails. "You did a good thing, dear," she says to me and smiles coyly. "I'm ninety years old. I was ninety yesterday." I smile back at her. "You look fantastic," I say. "Not a day over seventy-five." Her eyes flash. "Don't get smart," she says curtly.

At a coffee counter two women sit talking at right angles to me. One is telling the other that an older woman she knows is sleeping with a much younger man. "All her friends keep saying to her, 'He wants your money.'" The woman at the counter nods her head like a rag doll and lets her face go daffy in imitation of the woman she's speaking of. "'Right,' she tells them. 'And he can *have* it. *All* of it.' Meanwhile, she looks great."

At Forty-eighth Street a couple catches my eye. His face is ghastly white, hers a mask of badly applied make-up. Their eyes are swollen slits inside pouches of alcoholic skin. Both are wearing tight cheap clothes, her hips bursting from the skirt, his belly pushing up beneath the T-shirt. She bends with a cigarette in her mouth to take a light from the match in his trembling hand. As I pass them she straightens up, exhales her first breath of smoke, and says, "You are starting with a negative attitude. That is not the way to do it."

The streets attest to the power of narrative drive: its infinite capacity for adaptation in the most inhospitable of times. Civilization is breaking up? The city is deranged? The century is surreal? Move faster. Find the story line more quickly.

I cut over to Broadway and continue on downtown. At Forty-second Street, crossing in a mob of people, the man in front of me—skinny, black, young—suddenly lies down spread-eagled in the middle of the street just as the cars are beginning to move. I turn wildly to the man walking beside

me who, as it happens, is also skinny, young, black, and say to
him, "Why is he *doing* this?" Without breaking his stride he
shrugs at me, "I don't know, lady. Maybe he's depressed."

Each day when I leave the house I tell myself I'm going to
walk up the East Side of town because the East Side is calmer,
cleaner, more spacious, easier to stride about in. Yet, I seem
always to find myself on the crowded, filthy, volatile West
Side. I don't exactly know why this happens, but more often
than not an afternoon on the West Side feels positively the-
matic. All that intelligence trapped inside all those smarts. It
reminds me of why I walk. Why everyone walks.

Leonard and I are passing a bakery window on the Upper
East Side. Behind the shining plate glass stands a dishful of
madeleines.

"I've never had one," I say. "What are they like?"

"Nice," he replies. "Spongy," he adds. "Nothing to write six
novels about," he concludes.

We stop in front of a bookstore window with a display in it
of a book on cosmetic surgery written by a woman I know.

"She's only forty-two," I say. "Why is she writing about cosmetic surgery?"

"Maybe she's seventy," Leonard says. "What do you know?"

Two very thin men go by behind us. One is saying to the
other, "She gave a presentation on Jean Harris in jail, said she's
teaching sex education to the girls. What could Jean Harris
have to say about sex education?"

"Lesson number one," Leonard says to their retreating

backs. "Never give the man the gun, darlings. Remember: the man never gets the gun."

In the evening we have dinner at the home of a pair of lawyers we both know only slightly. The people at the table are homophobic, worshipful of "values," and avid to talk culture. The dinner is expensive but the conversation is junk food. The lawyers address themselves exclusively to me. I feel trapped. Repeatedly, I turn to Leonard to enjoy myself but I am alone at the table. He has withdrawn into a remoteness I cannot penetrate. Later, we walk through the dark and silent streets. The night is cold. We burrow into ourselves. After a time Leonard says to me, "I don't interest them. And the part of me that's interesting frightens them."

We do not draw closer because of what he has just said— I've been alone in his presence too many hours now—but life feels easier to bear for the clarity his words have imposed on an otherwise meaningless evening.

There isn't a neighborhood in New York that is free of the poor, the raffish, the unwanted. Social fluidity in the city means no one gets away from no one. Everywhere the avenues are made garish with the life of the streets. Nevertheless, neighborhoods accumulate personalities. Park Avenue still means rich, West End Avenue still means bourgeois. When I think of uptown I think of class.

The building I live in is a high rise in Greenwich Village. Like all high rises, it is stocked with a population the size of a town. The character of this population remains stable although its surface breaks up from time to time. When I first came to live here I thought I'd moved into a Dorothy Parker play: so many aging women, thin and alcoholic, with corkscrew curls and small dogs, hanging about in the lobby or the mailroom. One by one, the old women disappeared and were replaced by mournful-looking gay men who, one by one, have also disappeared. Now, it seems to me, there are a great number of people in the building like myself whose social stereotype is harder to reduce but who all live alone, and who all come and go with an air of preoccupied busyness that is, somehow, not persuasive.

Among the people I ride up and down in the elevator with is a couple I've never spoken to, although we always nod our heads in each other's direction. The woman has an Ellen Barkin mashed-in face and shoe-polish black hair; the man is blond, his face surgically smooth. They both wear black trenchcoats year in year out and are continually, even in the elevator, linked arm in arm. There's something uncanny about the way they adjust themselves to each other's movements. Sometimes I spot these two on the street, or even in other neighborhoods, walking with their faces turned straight out, not talking, welded together, grimly sealed off from all other human influence.

Last night I came home around 10:30. I turned the lights on in the apartment, listened to my phone messages, and was about to get undressed when I remembered I'd forgotten milk and oranges for the morning. I got back into my coat, walked out of the apartment, took the elevator down, and as I started across the lobby I saw a woman beating her head into her hand at the doorman's desk. It was the woman with the Ellen Barkin face. I stopped. "What is it?" I asked. She lifted her head, her face streaming tears, and cried out at me, "He just died! He died! In the *ambulance*. We didn't even get ta the hospital." "Omigod," I said and opened my arms to her. She fell into them, and as her head hit my shoulder I felt repelled. She did too. We each pulled away at the same instant. In her tough New York voice she said, "Sorry. Didn' mean ta fall apaht on ya." Her face was streaming. I shook my head to indicate it was nothing. She smiled at me. "He was a sweet man. We were happy." Her face caved in again. She cried out, "What am I gonna do? I never spent one night alone in my life!" I stood silent. She wiped her face, apologized again. Then she said to me, "What am I gonna do?" I looked into her eyes. "You'll figure it out," I said. She shrugged and walked toward the elevator. I turned and went out into the night.

Thirty years ago Greenwich Village was bohemia. It remains, to this day, the neighborhood of the peculiarly responsive and the oddly attached. When I was in my twenties, and hanging out at Village bars, I might have known the oddly attached would be a woman with an Ellen Barkin face beating her head at the doorman's desk. I never dreamed it was going to be me as well.

I live in the Village by default. It's not that the Village has a real personality anymore, it doesn't. Its personality evaporated the day bohemia ended, and it's lost territory as well, hemmed in now by dereliction on Eighth Street and tourism on Hudson. I live here because I feel uncomfortable elsewhere. Whatever the Village is or is not these days, it's still not class.

It's the hottest July on record, and I'm walking down Madison Avenue at two in the afternoon. Somewhere in the Forties I decide to get a frozen yogurt. As I walk out of the store the cone in my hand begins to melt. I stand there, licking as fast as I can. People start moving around me. I lick faster, but I'm not making any headway. The stuff is dripping down my hand onto the sidewalk. "Whatsamatta?" a man's voice says in my left ear, "don't you know how to eat an ice cream cone?" I turn, laughing, toward my interlocutor. He's small, dark, bearded, a manila envelope in his hand, and a big grin that dies on this mouth when he sees my face. "Ya not Susan Goldberg!" he cries as though I've deceived him. "I thought you was Susan Goldberg." His voice is half accusing, half apologetic. "Ya look just like Susan Goldberg. I mean, the eyes, the hair, the whole thing." I've got one eye on him, one on the melting yogurt. I'm still licking as fast as I can. I see the hair is matted, the beard scraggly, the eyes destroyed. "I wouldna talked ta ya if I'd known you wasn't Susan Goldberg," he goes on, "but I mean Susan Goldberg, she's a woman you don' wanna pass up, you know what I mean? You pass up Susan Goldberg she takes it personally. She thinks you don' like her. I got myself in a lotta trouble passing her up, but believe me, if I'd known you wasn't Susan Goldberg I wouldna talked ta ya."

Where are you sleeping tonight? I find myself thinking.

"That Susan Goldberg!" His laugh is crazy now. "She's really something." He shivers in the heat. "She reminds me of my mother."

In the park? the subway? can you hold it together until dark?

The grin returns to his mouth as suddenly as it left. "Anyway, you're a lot nicer than Susan Goldberg. Enjoy your ice cream cone!" He waves the manila envelope at me and dives into a building entrance a few doors away. I want to call after him, "It's not ice cream," but not having spoken a word it seems inappropriate to break my silence now.

I'm still standing there, paralyzed by the dripping cone. In less than a minute the small, dark man pops out of the building again, the manila envelope still in his hand: wrong address. He calls out, "Lady, enjoy ya-self!" grinning madly at me. "That's right, lady. Enjoy ya-self. Who knows how long we got, ya know what I mean?" I do not respond. But response is not required. All that is required is that I remain in place. He backtracks until he's standing beside me.

"You remind me of my mother," he says. "I love that woman. God, do I love that woman. I can't go see her, she lives in a bad neighborhood, ya know what I mean? I mean drugs an' all, it's no good for me, ya know what I mean? I'm so messed up right now, I mean I got all this pressure in my head, ya know what I mean, the drugs are no good, I mean I already lost two kids of my own by two women. I can't go see my mother, but I love that woman, I love her, I sent her an engagement ring, it ain't that I wanna make it with my mother, that's not what I mean, it ain't that, I sent her the ring ta let her know I got the *feelings,* ah, but it's no good for me I can't go see her, the neighborhood messes me up, an' I got all this pressure in my head."

By now I'm covered with dried drippings. My hand is stiffening into a chocolate-covered claw. I am subsiding into melted yogurt desperation. I'm as trapped by the indignity I've inflicted on myself as the man before me is by the pressure in his head. "Gee," he now says to me, "ya like a psychiatrist, ya know what I mean?"

"No," I say, driven at last to speak. "I *don't* know what you mean."

"Well," he says, "ya hangin' in there with me, listenin' ta me, tawkin' ta me." He giggles. "Just like one of them doctors on TV."

"I'm not doing anything!" I cry out. "You're doing it all yourself."

His head lolls idiotically on his shoulder. "Nah," he says, and explains patiently to me, "Ya lettin' me tawk. That's like tawkin' ta me."

Leonard and I are having tea at his house. I am sitting in the tall gray velvet chair, he across from me on the brown canvas couch.

"The other day," I tell him, "I was accused of being judgmental. What a laugh, I thought, you should have known me ten years ago. But, you know," I lean forward, "I'm *tired* of apologizing for being judgmental. Why *shouldn't* I be judgmental? I *like* being judgmental. Judgment is reassuring. Absolutes. Certainties. How I have loved them. I want them back again. Can't I have them back again?"

Leonard laughs and drums his fingers restlessly along the wooden armrest of his beautiful couch.

"Everyone used to seem grown up," I say. "Nobody does anymore. Look at us. Forty years ago we would have been our parents. Who are we now?"

He gets up and crosses the room to a closed cabinet, opens it and takes out a torn package of cigarettes. My eyes follow him in surprise. "What are you doing?" I say. "You've stopped smoking." He shrugs and extracts a cigarette from the package.

"They passed," Leonard said. "That's all. Forty years ago you entered a closet called marriage. In the closet was a double set of clothes, so stiff they could stand up by themselves. A woman stepped into the dress called 'wife' and a man stepped into a suit called 'husband.' And that was it. They disappeared inside the clothes." He strikes a match and holds it to his cigarette. "Today we don't pass. We're standing here naked. That's all." He drags on the cigarette. I watch him smoke for the first time in months.

"I'm not the right person for this life," I say.

"Who is?" he says, exhaling in my direction.

* * *

At Twenty-ninth Street two men wearing denim work shirts, dungarees, and hobnailed boots are walking beside me. Their eyes are blue, their necks are red, their bodies hard and narrow.

"Hey, how's your new place?" one asks the other.

"Great," comes the ready reply.

"What kinda furniture you got up there now?"

"Ah, it's terrific. I got a beautiful black leather couch. . ."

"No kidding."

"Of course my car's without a back seat now."

"I gotta come up there for dinner," the friend laughs.

"Yeah, sure. And bring a dinner with you."

The first man cuffs the second on the back of the head. The other puts up his fists, boxer style. The two start dancing about on the street as though they're in the ring together. They jab, they feint, they punch. The mimicry is perfect, astonishing in its detail and its concentration. Within seconds their bodies are made beautiful by the miracle of purpose and control. I know, given the wrong time on the right street, in Brooklyn or in Queens, these two could turn murderous, but right now they're masters of an art, performing at full strength, transforming the open pavement into a piece of theater.

At Thirty-third Street a truck starts across Fifth Avenue just as the light is about to change. Instant gridlock. A woman standing beside me at the curb turns to me and in the accents of my childhood says, "Can you buh-*leeve* this? He noo he couldn't clear the aven-noo!" I look at her like an archeologist returning to the sound of a language she did her thesis on. I know this street-wise primitive so well. It doesn't matter if I respond to her or not. If I don't, someone on the next corner will. She knows that, and I know that. But it is my intense and bottomless pleasure to match my voice to hers and shaking my head say, as though between her ejaculation and my replay not a day has separated us from our mutual history, "No. I don't buh-leeve it."

At Forty-second Street two women and three children stand motionless beside an open hot dog counter. The children, two boys and a girl, are looking gloomy, the women distressed. One woman is angry, the other one miserable. The angry one says, "*Why* I say that? I say that because they *in-*grates! *That's* why I say that." The unhappy one does not reply. As I pass them the oldest boy, holding a soda can in his hand, begins dancing around the others. "You just a bunch of lil' ingrates," he chants softly into the girl's ear, using the straw in his can to jab at her.

At Forty-ninth Street I board the crosstown bus. Every seat is taken. At the back I come to a halt in front of a woman who, along with her packages, occupies two spaces. She wears a black dress, black high-heeled shoes, and a black picture hat. The lines in her face are made deep by heavy make-up, her eye shadow is smeared, and lipstick has made its way into the creases around her mouth. The packages are three Lord and Taylor shopping bags. Beside me stands a woman about the age of the woman in the picture hat. She is stocky, her hair is gray and cropped like Gertrude Stein's, the eyes behind steel-rimmed glasses blue, placid, intelligent. She looks thoughtfully at the packages and leans forward. "Would you mind removing your things from the seat?" she asks in a kindly voice. "I'd like to sit down." The woman in the hat nods slowly. She seems to be gathering herself together to remove the bags but two blocks later they're still on the seat. She receives an inquiring look. "You're rushing me!" she says loudly. "I won't tolerate it." Gertrude Stein leans back on her low brown heels, taking the measure of the woman in the hat. "We ain't none of us getting any younger, lady," she says, her voice dangerously soft. "Move the fucking packages."

Later in the day I walk to the corner for cash. As I approach the bank I see a man up against the building, face to the wall, surrounded by uniformed police. I make my way around the cops, plastic card in hand, and push inside. The line is short. Everyone on it stares languidly out at the street. In front of the money machine a woman punches furiously at the keys on the flat plastic surface.

"They must have nothing to do," a schoolgirl in front of me says. "Fifteen cops and just this one guy."

"Right," the man in front of her says. "You know how much this little scene is costing the city?"

The girl shrugs. "Maybe he's bionic man," she says.

Outside, two policemen jerk the rebellious captive up against the window.

The door flies open. An anorexic man stands in the doorway, card in hand, alarm in his eyes. "He didn't rob *this* place, did he?"

"No," we all chorus. "Come on in. Money for everyone."

The woman at the machine turns away defeated. "Money for everyone," she grins at the line, "except that poor bastard out there and me."

In the evening I have dinner at my table looking out at the city. As the sky darkens and the lights begin to go on in the buildings all around I see, in the air between me and the crowded horizon, the people of the day. I remember the boy with the jabbing soda can, the woman with the Lord and Taylor shopping bags. I laugh to myself as I hear again the words they spoke, see their faces and gestures. I begin revising the scenes, adding dialogue here, analysis there, commentary further on. Then I find myself backing up, imagining each of them before we met up. With a start, I realize I am writing the story of the day, lending shape and texture to the hours just behind me. They're in the room with me now, these people I brushed against today. They've become company, great company. I'd rather be here with them tonight than with anyone else I know. They return the narrative impulse to me. Let me make sense of things. Remind me to tell the story I cannot make my life tell.

I need them. I need the Bronx primitive on Thirty-third, Gertrude Stein on the bus, bionic man in the bank. I need them more than I need clean air, safe streets, or low taxes. I need them, and I have them. If everyone I know died tomor-

row I'd still have them. I'd have the city. I smile into the dark.
I'm happy. Happy and relieved. Relieved and free. I feel free.
Free to begin and end with myself. Free to imagine tomorrow.

The telephone rings. It's Leonard.

"Hello!" I say.

"*You* sound up," he says.

I laugh.

"Are we getting together this week?" he asks.

"Yes, of course."

"There's a new English movie I want to see."

"Fine."

"Two gays get arrested in Berlin."

"What could be better?"

2 the catskills remembered

I HAVE NEVER BEEN ABLE TO THINK OF the old Catskill Mountains hotel circuit as the actual setting for all those borscht belt jokes. For me, a college student waitressing in the late fifties, the Catskills was a wild place, dangerous and exciting, where all the beasts were predatory, none pacific. The years I spent working in those hotels were my introduction to the brutishness of function, the murderousness of fantasy, the isolation inflicted on all those living inside a world organized to provide pleasure. It's the isolation I've been thinking about lately—how remarkably present it was, crude and vibrant, there from the first moment of contact.

I walked into Stella Mercury's employment agency one afternoon in the winter of my freshman year at City College.

30

Four men sat playing cards with a greasy deck, chewing gum methodically, never looking up once. The woman at the desk, fat and lumpy with hard eyes and a voiceful of cigarette wheeze, said to me, "Where ya been?" and I rattled off a string of hotels. "Ya worked all those places," she said calmly. "Ain't the human body a mah-h-vellous thing, ya don't look old enough to have worked half of 'em." I stood there, ill with fear that on the one hand she'd throw me out and on the other she'd give me a job, and assured her that I had. She knew I was lying, and I knew that she knew I was lying, but she wrote out a job ticket anyway. Suddenly I felt lonely inside the lie, and I begged her with my eyes to acknowledge the truth between us. She didn't like that at all. Her own eyes grew even harder, and she refused me more than she had when I'd not revealed open need. She drew back with the ticket still in her hand. I snatched at it. She laughed a nasty laugh. And that was it, all of it, right there, two flights above Times Square, I was in the mountains.

That first weekend in a large glittering hotel filled with garment district salesmen and midtown secretaries, weaving clumsily in and out of the vast kitchen all heat and acrimony (food flying, trays crashing, waiters cursing), I gripped the tray so hard all ten knuckles were white for days afterward, and every time I looked at them I recalled the astonishment I'd felt when a busboy at the station next to mine stuck out his fist to a guest who'd eaten three main dishes and said, "Want a knuckle sandwich?" But on Sunday night when I flung fifty single dollar bills on the kitchen table before my open-mouthed mother there was soft exultancy, and I knew I'd go back. Rising up inside this brash, moralistic, working-class girl was the unexpected excitement of the first opportunity for greed.

I was eighteen years old, moving blind through hungers whose force I could not grasp. Unable to grasp what drove me, I walked around feeling stupid. Feeling stupid I became inept. Secretly, I welcomed going to the mountains. I knew I could do this hard but simple thing. I could enter that pig-eyed glitter and snatch from it the soft, gorgeous, fleshy excitement of quick money. This I could master. This, I thought, had only to do with endurance; inexhaustible energy; and that I was burning up with.

The summer of my initiation I'd get a job, work two weeks, get fired. "You're a waitress? I thought you said you were a waitress. What kinda waitress sets a table like that? Who you think you're kidding, girlie?" But by Labor Day I *was* a waitress and a veteran of the first year. I had been inducted into an underclass elite, a world of self-selected Orwellian pariahs for whom survival was the only value.

At the first hotel an experienced waiter, attracted by my innocence, took me under his wing. In the mountains, regardless of age or actual history, your first year you were a virgin and in every hotel there was always someone, sentimental as a gangster, to love a virgin. My patron in this instance was a twenty-nine-year-old man who worked in the post office in

winter and at this hotel in summer. He was a handsome va-
grant, a cunning hustler, what I would come by the end of the
summer to recognize as a "mountain rat."

One night a shot rang out in the sleeping darkness. Waiters
and waitresses leaped up in the little barracks building we
shared at the edge of the hotel grounds. Across the wide lawn,
light filled the open doorway of one of the distant guest cot-
tages. A man stood framed in the light, naked except for a
jockstrap. Inside the barracks people began to laugh. It was
my handsome protector. He'd been sleeping with a woman
whose gambler husband had appeared unexpectedly on a
Thursday night.

The next day he was fired. We took a final walk together. I
fumbled for words. Why? I wanted to know. I knew he didn't
like the woman, a diet-thin blonde twenty years older than
himself. "Ah-h-h," my friend said wearily. "Doncha know
nothing, kid? Doncha know what I am? I mean, whaddaya
think I am?"

At the second hotel the headwaiter, a tall sweating man, began all his staff meetings with, "Boys and girls, the first thing
to understand is, we are dealing here with animals." He stood
in the dining-room doorway every morning holding what I
took to be a glass of apple juice until I was told it was whiskey
neat. "Good morning, Mrs. Levine," he'd nod affably, then
turn to a busboy and mutter, "That Holland Tunnel whore."
He rubbed my arm between his thumb and his forefinger
when he hired me and said, "We'll take care of each other,

right, kid?" I nodded, thinking it was his way of asking me to be a responsible worker. My obtuseness derailed him. When he fired me and my friend Marilyn because he caught us eating chocolate tarts behind an alcove in the dining room he thundered at us, his voice hoarse with relief, "You are not now waitresses, you never were waitresses, you'll never *be* waitresses."

At the third hotel I had fifty dollars stolen from me at the end of a holiday weekend. Fifty dollars wasn't fifty dollars in the mountains, it was blood money. My room was crowded with fellow workers, all silent as pallbearers. The door racketed open and Kennie, a busboy who was always late, burst into the room. "I heard you had money stolen!" he cried, his face stricken. I nodded wordlessly. Kennie turned, pulled the door shut, twisted his body about, raised his arm and banged his fist, sobbing, against the door. When I said, "What are *you* getting so excited about?" he shrieked at me, "Because you're a waitress and a human being! And I'm a busboy and a human being!" At the end of the summer, four more robberies having taken place, the thief was caught. It was Kennie.

At the fourth hotel the children's waiter was a dedicated womanizer. A flirtatious guest held out on him longer than usual, and one morning I saw this waiter urinate into a glass of orange juice, then serve it to the woman's child with the crooning injunction to drink it all up because it was so-o-o good.

At the fifth hotel I served a woman who was all bosom from neck to knee, tiny feet daintily shod, smooth plump hands beautifully manicured, childish eyes in a painted face. When I brought her exactly-three-minute eggs to the table she said to me, "Open them for me, dear. The shells burn my hands." I turned away, to the station table against the wall, to perform in appropriate secrecy a task that told me for the first but certainly not the last time that here I was only an extension of my function. It was the Catskills, not early socialist teachings at my father's knee, that made me a Marxist.

One winter I worked weekends and Christmas at a famous hotel. This hotel had an enormous tiered dining room and was run by one of the most feared headwaiters in the mountains. The system here was that all newcomers began at the back of the dining room on the tier farthest from the kitchen. If your work met with favor you were moved steadily toward the center, closer to the kitchen doors and to the largest tips which came not from the singles who were invariably placed in the back of the room but from the middle-aged manufacturers, club owners, and gangsters who occupied the tables in the central tiers, cutting a wide swath as though across a huge belly between the upper and lower ends of the dining room.

As the autumn wore on I advanced down the tiers. By Christmas I was nearly in the center of the room, at one of the best stations in the house. This meant my guests were now middle-aged married couples whose general appearance was characterized by blond bouffants, mink stoles, midnight-blue suits, and half-smoked cigars. These people ate prodigiously and tipped well.

That Christmas the hotel was packed and we worked twelve hours a day. The meals went on forever. By the end of the week we were dead on our feet but still running. On New Year's Eve at midnight we were to serve a full meal, the fourth of the day, but this was to be a banquet dinner—that is, a series of house-chosen dishes simply hauled out, course by course—and we looked forward to it. It signaled the end of the holiday. The next morning the guests checked out and that night we'd all be home in our Bronx or Brooklyn apartments, our hard-earned cash piled on the kitchen table.

But a threatening atmosphere prevailed at that midnight meal from the moment the dining room doors were flung open. I remember sky blue sequined dresses and tight mouths, satin cummerbunds and hard-edged laughter, a lot of drunks on the vomitous verge. People darted everywhere and all at once, pushing to get at the central tables (no assigned seats tonight), as though, driven from one failed part of the evening to another here, at last, they were going to get what *should* come through for them: a good table in the famous dining room during its New Year's Eve meal.

The kitchen was instantly affected: it picked up on atmosphere like an animal whose only survival equipment is hyperalertness. A kind of panicky aggression seemed to overtake the entire staff. The orderly lines that had begun to form for the first appetizer broke almost immediately. People who had grown friendly, working together over these long winter weekends, now climbed over each other's backs to break into the line and grab at the small round dishes piled up on the huge steel tables.

I made my first trip into the kitchen, took in the scene before me, and froze. Then I took a deep breath, inserted myself into a line, held my own against hands and elbows pushing into my back and ribs, and got my tray loaded and myself out the kitchen doors. I served the fruit cup quickly and, depending on my busboy to get the empties off the tables in time, made my anxious way back into the kitchen for the next course which, I'll not forget as long as I live, was chow mein. This time I thought violence was about to break out. All those people, trays, curses being flung about! And now I couldn't seem to take a deep breath: I remained motionless just inside the kitchen doors. Another waitress, a classmate from City College, grabbed my arm and whispered in my ear, "Skip the chow mein, they'll never know the difference. Go on to the next course, there's nobody on the line over there." My heart lifted, the darkness receded. I stared at her. Did we dare? Yes, she nodded grimly, and walked away. It didn't occur to either of us to consider that she, as it happened, had only drunken singles at her tables who of course wouldn't know the difference, but I had married couples who wanted everything that was coming to them.

I made my first mistake. I followed my classmate to the table with no line in front of it, loaded up on the cold fish, and fought my way out the nearest kitchen door. Rapidly, I dealt out the little dishes to the men and women at my tables. When

I had finished and was moving back to my station table and its now empty tray, a set of long red fingernails plucked at my upper arm. I looked down at a woman with coarse blond hair, blue eyelids surrounded by lines so deep they seemed carved, and a thin red mouth. "We didn't get the chow mein," she said to me.

My second mistake. "Chow mein?" I said. "What chow mein?" Still holding me, she pointed to the next table where chow mein was being finished and the cold fish just beginning to be served. I looked at her. Words would not come. I broke loose, grabbed my tray, and dived into the kitchen.

I must have known I was in trouble because I let myself be kicked about in the kitchen madness, wasting all sorts of time being climbed over before I got the next dish loaded onto my tray and inched myself, crablike, through the swinging doors. As I approached my station I saw, standing beside the blond woman, the headwaiter, chewing a dead cigar and staring glumly in my direction. He beckoned me with one raised index finger.

I lowered my tray onto the station table and walked over to him. "Where's the chow mein?" he asked quietly, jerking his thumb back at my tables, across the head of the woman whose blue-lidded eyes never left his face. Her mouth was a slash of narrow red. Despair made me simple.

"I couldn't get to it." I said. "The kitchen is a madhouse. The line was impossible."

The headwaiter dropped his lower lip. His black eyes flickered into dangerous life and his hand came up slowly to re-move the cigar stub from between his teeth. "You couldn't *get* to it?" he said. "Did I hear you right? You said you couldn't get to it?" A few people at neighboring tables looked up.

"That's right," I said miserably.

And then he was yelling at me, "And you call yourself a waitress?"

A dozen heads swung around. The headwaiter quickly shut his mouth. He stared coldly at me, in his eyes the most ex-traordinary mixture of anger, excitement, and fear. Yes, fear. Frightened as I was, I saw that he too was afraid. Afraid of the blond woman who sat in her chair like a queen with the power of life and death in her, watching a minister do her awful bid-ding. His eyes kept darting toward her, as though to ask, All right? Enough? Will this do?

No, the unyielding face answered. Not enough. Not nearly enough.

"You're fired," the headwaiter said to me. "Serve your morning meal and clear out."

The blood seemed to leave my body in a single rush. For a moment I thought I was going to faint. Then I realized that to-morrow morning my regular guests would be back in these seats, most of them leaving after breakfast, and I, of course, would receive my full tips exactly as though none of this had happened. The headwaiter was not really punishing me. He knew it, and now I knew it. Only the blond woman didn't know it. She required my dismissal for the appeasement of her lousy life—her lined face, her hated husband, her disappointed New Year's Eve—and he, the headwaiter, was required to deliver it up to her.

For the first time I understood something about power. I stared into the degraded face of the headwaiter and saw that he was as trapped as I, caught up in a working life that required *someone's* humiliation at all times.

The summer I turned twenty-one I graduated both from City College and from the Catskills. It was an apotheosis that summer, that hotel: no one and nothing seemed small, simple, or real. The owners were embezzling the place, the headwaiter was on the take, the cook gave us food poisoning. The viciousness between busboys and waiters was more unrestrained than I had ever seen it and the waitresses were required to mingle, that is, show up in the casino at night and "dance" with the male guests, as the headwaiter leeringly put it.

The staff was filled with people I had worked with before, and two old friends were there as well: Marilyn of "you're not now waitresses" fame and Ricky, the waitress who had advised me to forget the chow mein. We three roomed together in a tiny barracks room inside of which was jammed four cots, four small chests of drawers, two narrow closets, and two rickety bedside tables.

The fourth bed in our room was occupied by Marie, a stranger to us in every way. From the moment I saw her sitting on the edge of her bed removing her stockings as Marilyn and I came in from the first lunch meal of an early June weekend I knew she was not like us. I knew it from the way she was taking off her stockings. Our hands would have torn quickly at the stocking, pulling it off in one swift gesture, hers moved slowly over leg and stocking together; the motion they made was one that prolonged the moment rather than telescoped it, the expression on her face sensual not impatient.

She was tall and thin, one of those women with narrow shoulders, small breasts, a high waist and long legs who, even when she gains weight, looks slim: the kind of body that is never stylish, always alluring. Her hair, as unfashionable as her body, was a long red frizz that clung in Botticelli curls about her face and forehead and straggled down her back in a ragged ponytail. The eyes were large, the nose bony, the skin milk white. Her mouth, easily her most distinctive feature, was long with deep creases in the lips. ("Ravaged" was the word that, with an unexpected thrill, came into my head.) We all smoked, but she chain-smoked. Those lips came with a cigarette between them.

The three of us were twenty-one, Marie was twenty-five. We were students, she was an out-of-work actress. We were old hands in the mountains, she was a novice. We lived at home with our working-class families, she came from a middle-class family with whom she had severed relations. She was an unknown: I could not imagine her before she came among us and I could not imagine her after she'd leave us. No, I take that back. It wasn't that I couldn't imagine her, it was that it didn't occur to me to imagine her.

In the mountains only that which caused blunt outrage or

open despair (bad tips, an intractable busboy, unhappy sex, a strained back) attracted deeper attention. If someone was not directly responsible for anger or misery the instinct to speculate was not aroused. Like the dining room furniture, the kitchen heat, or the heavy trays, people were simply "there," part of a vast set against which we moved without nuance or dimension.

The waiter at the station next to mine that summer was another social oddity: Vinnie Liebowitz, an ambitious pre-med student whose name wasn't Liebowitz at all, it was Lentino. But as Vinnie said, "Who could make out in the Catskills with a name like Lentino?" and making out was what Vinnie was all about.

Vinnie was a smart, well-organized waiter who while not expansive was not excessively guarded either. A once dedicated seducer of women, he had never been driven by the intense need to score that dominated all sexual transactions in the mountains. He thought of himself as having a tender rather than a fierce appetite for the act of love.

In his second year in the mountains Vinnie had met Carol, a girl whose conventional good looks matched his own to an uncanny extent: same chiseled features, same large brown eyes and dense black hair, same thin, self-regarding body. Vinnie had pursued Carol madly. She had expertly beckoned and avoided him. By the end of that summer they were engaged. The plan was to marry after Vinnie's first year in medical school.

Vinnie and Carol had not slept together and were not going to until their wedding night. In this, the third summer of engagement, their passionate necking sessions had become regulated, and they found themselves absorbed by the more mature considerations of life; such as, where they would make their future home (Brooklyn or Long Island), the kind of furniture they would have, number of babies, location of summer and winter vacations. Vinnie was sometimes baffled as to how it was that his entire life seemed settled at the age of twenty-two, but he was working class from Brooklyn and Carol was a princess from Forest Hills. Without her, he often said, he'd have spent the rest of his life pumping gas in Brownsville.

All this I knew because that summer Carol and her parents were guests at a hotel fifteen miles from ours where my boyfriend Danny was working as a busboy, and two or three times a week Vinnie (the only waiter with a car) drove over to see Carol and took me along. This boyfriend of mine was also a medical student and a man of good-natured appetite as well. Danny loved sex, food, jazz, and memorizing medical textbooks. He also thought he loved me. And sometimes I thought the same. Together, we'd been meeting the needs of the moment for more than a year now.

The summer wore on in an exhaustion that came early and stayed late. By the end of July, young and healthy as we were, tiredness began dissolving collectively into all of us. People fell asleep sitting on the toilet, or standing on line in the kitchen, or taking a shower. One afternoon Marilyn got down on her hands and knees to retrieve a shoe that had been kicked under her cot; no sooner was her head parallel with the floor than her body forgot why it was there, and she fell asleep.

I don't think any of us ever felt lonely. Hot, angry, bored, weary yes, but lonely? No. Partly it was that punishing physical labor precludes every kind of reflectiveness, including the one out of which loneliness arises; partly it was that we lived in a mob scene, and the absence of solitude obscures the issue. But even at the time neither condition seemed fully to explain our uniform disallowance of this particular emotion.

One morning at seven o'clock, as I was walking from the barracks to the kitchen door, I stopped to smell the air on the great hotel lawn. The moment was lovely: clear and sensual. Buried in the early morning cool was the growing heat that would spread itself hour by hour across the sexy summer day. I felt pierced to the heart. There were other ways to spend this day! Other lives to live, other people to be. I did then what was never done: I began to daydream. I saw myself standing in the same morning light somewhere else, under a great shade tree of a kind we didn't have in the mountains. Beside me, on the grass, sat a group of strangers—graceful, beautiful, intelligent—animated by clever talk and sophisticated laughter. They invited me to join them, even made a place for me on the grass. I longed to sit down. I felt that I *knew* these people, that I belonged among them. Suddenly and without warning, a space seemed to open between me and the image in my mind. The space lengthened into a road. It was clear that I would have to walk the road, step by step, to get to my people. The movie in my mind stopped running. I could not *see* myself on the road. I could not imagine the steps, taken one by one, that were necessary to close the gap between me and the people I was daydreaming. Inside, I began to congeal. Then all inner movement ceased. I stood on the lawn and stared at my own dumb longing. Desolation crowded in. I was lonely.

I remember that I wrenched myself then from the loneliness. It frightened me. I had felt myself pitching forward, as though about to lose my balance. And balance, I knew, was everything. I looked around me at the lawn, the buildings, the parking lot, this small, tight world where function was all, and I had learned to operate supremely well (avoid gross humiliation and control the limits of surrender). All I had to do was look straight ahead, keep my mouth shut, and my balance intact. Life, I thought grimly, whatever its size or composition, depends on walking the straight and narrow of the moment. I turned away from my own daydream and walked through the kitchen door.

Yet everything seemed harder than ever that summer. The tips were bad, the cook was a sadist, and we had to steal more meat, fruit, and milk than usual. The mountains were always one long siege of vitamin deprivation. No one ever wanted to feed the help; the agony on an owner's face if his eye fell on a busboy drinking orange juice or eating a lamb chop was palpable. One night a waiter was fired because the maitre d' tore open his bulging shirt as he was leaving the dining room and found two steaks lying flat against his naked chest. Six or eight of us watched from our stations. No one spoke, no one moved. What made things worse in this instance was that many of us knew the maitre d' was out to fire this waiter because he had refused to kick back.

The headwaiter was a Hungarian Jew with a despairing sense of class: life had dealt him a blow by making him end his working years in the mountains. A vain handsome man, all brushed white hair, manicured hands, and sky blue suits to match the color of his eyes, he perspired constantly and, if taken by surprise, his eyes rolled in his head. He often began staff meetings with a hysterical denunciation of these rumors about pay-offs that his enemies (and don't think for a minute he didn't know who *they* were) were spreading. Most of us sat at these meetings genuinely baffled by such ravings, but some of us nodded our heads in vigorous sympathy for the injustices suffered by the sweating madman who paced the floor in front of us. Those of us who were baffled were indeed in the dark, those of us who were nodding were regularly handing over 10 percent of our tips to be assured a full station each week.

In mid-August fifteen people came down with food poisoning. The huskiest waiters in the hotel were clutching their stomachs and heaving into their busboys' dish bins. One of them vomited all night, another was delirious for twelve hours, a third drooled up green bile. The barracks took on the hushed atmosphere of an epidemic ward. When we discovered that the source of the food poisoning had been a dinner made up of turkey wings the cook suspected of having gone bad one of the waitresses broke. The cook had been making her life miserable, grabbing at her, taunting her, and now, her body racked with diarrhetic convulsion, she demanded and gained entry to the owner's office. He sat behind his desk. Beside him stood his son and the bell captain. The waitress began to speak. She told her story of weariness and harassment and then described in detail how those poisoned were suffering. She demanded the dismissal of the cook. The owner stared into a space somewhere between her shoulder and the door. "Get this cunt outta here," he announced to the air. Stunned, the waitress allowed herself to be led, as though blind, from the office. In the barracks she told what had happened. Some of us were silent, some of us cursed, some turned quickly away. Needless to say, no one did anything.

My visits to Danny were, during these days, a consolation. I was grateful to him for providing me with a means of escape from the hotel. It was not only being with Danny that made going to see him important, it was everything about the visit itself—hurrying to get out of the dining room on the nights I knew we were traveling, climbing into Vinnie's car with the smell of summer stronger than when I was going nowhere, driving through the dark silent countryside behind the sweep of headlights beyond which the familiar daytime roads and hotels had become almost mysterious.

The night was invariably rich, dark, sweet, shot through with a kind of lit-from-within intensity. The smell of wet earth came up through grass, trees swayed in a warm wind, molecules of excitement gathered in the clear mountain air. Sitting close together on the front seat of his ten-year-old Chevy, Vinnie and I were both infected by the atmosphere.

Aroused in each other's presence, we hardly ever thought we were being aroused by each other, yet this closeness, which blossomed only on the ride out never on the way back, began to accumulate a peculiar life. We never spoke of it, and certainly we did not bring it back with us to the hotel. Nonetheless, I felt its influence. Sometimes, something ordinary came into unexpected relief and suddenly the familiar would seem threatening. I'd feel a shock to the system, and I'd find myself flashing on the ride out with Vinnie.

Take Marilyn and the butcher, for instance. This butcher, a good-looking ex-Marine, was a true primitive: murderous when crossed, slavishly loyal when done a good turn. In his lexicon Marilyn had done him a good turn by bestowing the gift of her virginity on him, and his devotion knew no bounds. He assured her daily he would steal and kill for her.

Marilyn, of course, had a hard time concentrating on Thomas's adoration as her virginity had been an obstacle to "getting on with it," and she was grateful to Tom for relieving her of its burdensomeness. The most hardened mountain rat participated in a fear of virginity, and every one of them had drawn back from the taint of Marilyn's purity. Thomas also had drawn back but she had been able to persuade him that her feeling for him was so deep it would be a sin *not* to. To this argument he finally assented and thereafter treated Marilyn worshipfully, her capacity for such deep feeling, coupled with the contradictory reference to sin, having become confused in him with religious experience.

Thomas appeared regularly in our room after dinner and while Marilyn lay back on her bed, still in her work clothes, he would sit dreamily stroking her lower leg. As he did so the secret smile that seemed perpetually on Marilyn's mouth these days deepened and, beneath the dirty white uniform, a long delicate shudder moved visibly down the length of her beautiful midriff and flat belly. She had become sleek as a bird-eating cat since she'd begun making love, and almost as remote.

One afternoon I came into the room after the lunch meal and saw the *Times* lying on Marilyn's bed. Surprised, as we never got the papers, I said, "Where'd this come from?" Marilyn followed my eyes to the bed. "Oh, Tom left it here this morning," she said. My eyebrows went up. "Thomas reads the *Times?*" I asked. Marilyn's face turned a dull red. "He does *now,*" she said. Her eyes came up level with mine. We looked at each other for a long suspended moment. Then we both began to howl.

Suddenly I felt gripped with anxiety, and in my mind's eye I saw me and Vinnie riding through the night toward who, what, I didn't know. But this, me and Marilyn laughing over Thomas, it frightened me. Something vicious here, something fearful and sacrificial. My heart pressed on my ribs.

Three weeks before Labor Day Vinnie and I climbed into

the Chevy one night and took off. We'd been late getting out of the dining room, and now Vinnie was driving fast. As he raced along the road he could drive in his sleep, I babbled at him a tale of dining-room fatigue having to do with a guest I'd spilled hot liquid on three meals in a row. The story had a point, and I was reaching it. Vinnie leaned forward over the wheel, his fine black eyebrows pressing closer together over the bridge of his thin straight nose, his wonderfully dark eyes narrowed with concentration. Just as I was about to deliver the punch line, the car swerved sharply to the right of the road and came to an abrupt halt.

Vinnie turned to me. Even in the dark I could see how white his face had become. His eyes were a film of misery. We stared at one another.

"I can't stand it anymore," he whispered.

"Stand what?" I whispered back

"I want her," he moaned.

"Carol, you mean?"

"No. Marie!"

"Marie?" I repeated.

"Yes."

"Marie from our hotel?"

"Yes!"

"But you're engaged to Carol," I explained.

"I know!" he cried. "Don't you think I know that? Don't you think I say to myself every day and every night, You've got Carol. Carol who loves you, Carol who's a thousand times better looking than she is, a thousand times sharper, nicer, more terrific in every way. But it doesn't do any good. I want *her*. And it's tearing me apart!"

I could feel my eyes growing large in the dark. "How long has this been going on?" I asked, my voice nakedly curious.

"Weeks," he said, slumping back against the seat. He stared bleakly out the window. "It feels like years but I guess it's really only weeks."

"Does she know?"

"I'm not sure. I think so. But I'm not sure."

"You mean you've never said anything to her?"

"Christ, no. To begin with, I couldn't believe this was happening to me, and then. . ." The color was returning to his cheeks. "I was confused and ashamed. Jesus Christ. Marie! She's not good-looking, she's older than me, she's like no one I ever knew." His voice broke. "I mean sometimes she really looks like hell." He stopped talking. I waited. When he spoke again his voice was soft and steady. "I don't know how it started," he said. "One day I was just aware of her. Aware of her in the kitchen. Aware of her in the dining room. Aware of her in the barracks. Aware her. Once we both reached into the silverware pail at the same time. My hand touched hers and I felt like I'd been burned. I was so surprised. I didn't know what it meant. After that I'd find myself looking for her in the dining room. And all this time I'm saying to myself, Vinnie you crazy? What's goin' on here? Remember Carol? The girl you love. The girl you're gonna marry. The best-looking girl in the mountains. What *is* this? But it didn't do any good. Every day I'd find myself thinking about *her.* More and more. Not exactly thinking about her, just *feeling* her, feeling her presence, and then I couldn't take my eyes off her when she was anywhere near me." He struck his forehead with his balled-up right hand and fell forward over the wheel. "She *must* know," he groaned. "I can't figure out how come everybody doesn't know. I feel like it's written all over my face all the time."

"It's not," I said drily.

His long speech had given me time to absorb what he was saying, but I too kept repeating to myself, Marie? Carol is so beautiful, so right in every way. What has *Marie* got to do with anything? I could not take it in. Handsome, pre-med Vinnie Liebowitz, with this life all mapped out, wanting Marie who in no way belonged. It was crazy, nuts, exciting. That was another thing I couldn't take in: I was excited by Vinnie's confession of desire for Marie.

"I feel better for having told you," Vinnie smiled wanly. "You don't mind, do you? I mean, you're not sorry I told you, are you?"

"Of course not," I said briskly, not knowing what I felt. "But we'd better go now. They'll be waiting for us."

Vinnie's eyes clouded over. He nodded at me and turned the key in the ignition. The car climbed back onto the road. In twenty minutes we were pulling into the driveway of Carol and Danny's hotel.

I remember lying in Danny's arms that night fantasizing

about Vinnie and Marie. I saw them locked together, thrashing wildly, their faces contorted with pain, their bodies in fever. My own body was so coiled with tension that Danny's pleasure was greatly heightened, and he suggested we might be falling in love anew. I said nothing. I could hardly hear his voice, my attention had wandered so far from the man I was lying with. It was a relief, two hours later, to be back in the car where burning interest could be openly pursued. The ride home was spent with me pumping Vinnie about Marie, and he plunging eagerly into his tale of illicit desire.

After that night our rides took on new meaning. Vinnie's obsession had touched something secret in him, and a strain of wildness had flared in us both. When I had daydreamed my beautiful people, the clever ones, the ones I couldn't reach on my own, the fantasy had made me lonely. But now, daydreaming Vinnie and Marie, there rose up in me a hunger so open and so acute it sent me into a trance. Reckless, sweet, compelling, it became a dream that settled in the groin. Vinnie's desire became all desire, his urgency all urgency, his necessity a drama we could, neither of us, get enough of. I felt released into complicity, about what I did not know. I only knew that the atmosphere inside the car had become rich with secrecy. He talked, and I fed him questions. My questions extended the obsession, deepened the drama. Some live, fluid movement went streaking through our furtive exchange. A wave of hidden promise rose and fell in the speeding dark, and rose again. I wanted to go on riding it forever.

I could imagine for him what I could not imagine for myself, and often what I imagined felt alarming: hard, bright, insistent. This was the exact opposite of my lonely daydream. This was all appetite and acquisition; what triggered everyone around me. It appalled and excited me. I remember once flashing on the woman who'd gotten me fired that long ago New Year's Eve. Suddenly I could feel her mean hungriness moving inside me. I wanted Vinnie to get what he wanted the way she had wanted to get . . . what? What was it exactly that she *had* wanted to get? At this point my thoughts went fuzzy, but the feeling remained: hard and bright. The trance deepened. Nothing seemed to matter then, only that desire be gratified.

One night we got into the car and Vinnie said to me, "Talk to her." I fell toward him as though I'd been slapped and had involuntarily jerked the wrong way. "What do mean, talk to her? And say what?" He was silent, his handsome face white and drawn. "Tell her how I feel," he said. "I can't do it, I just can't do it. And you could. I mean, you're a girl, you live with her, you're sort of friends. You could explain it to her. Ask her to meet me after the meal tomorrow night. Just that. Nothing else. She's got nothing to be afraid of. Tell her that. I won't hurt her, I won't ask her to do anything she doesn't want to do. I just want to talk to her." He brightened up. "That's all," he repeated. "I just want to talk to her. She's got nothing to be afraid of. Nothing. I swear it."

My heart began to pound. I slept beside Marie every night

but she was not as real to me in the flesh as she was here in the car, a conjured vision, the shared object of Vinnie's over-excited anguish. I stared at him. I yearned to remain as we were, locked together inside the nighttime confessional of the car, and I think he did too. I saw that he was afraid yet he felt compelled to act, to move into consequence.

He lifted his head high in the darkened car, his eyes pinpoints of dilated light, his jawline a throb of congested strain. Then his head dropped forward over his smooth, beautiful neck. Humbled by need, he had become unbearably handsome.

"I'll talk to her," I said.

The next morning as we were stumbling around getting ready for breakfast I asked Marie to meet with me after the meal. She looked quizzically at me, but I remained silent. "Sure," she said quietly. We each turned back into ourselves, finished dressing, and tore out of the room.

Four hours later Marie and I walked through the dining room doors together for the first time that summer and headed wordlessly for the pool. This was a "singles" hotel; at 10:30 in the morning, we knew, there would be no one lying on the painted concrete beside the chlorine blue water. As we walked I glanced at Marie's bare legs. They were scruffy looking, in need of a shave. For the thousandth time I thought, "Why her? Why does he want her?"

We sat down on the lower ends of two lounge chairs, uneasy in our occupancy (we never used guest facilities), and faced each other across the black-and-white expanse of our morning uniforms. Marie seemed not tense but alert, her long narrow body waiting, her bony face a smooth mask. Suddenly I was overcome with confusion. Why was I about to speak of intimate matters for one stranger with another stranger? I did then what I always did in confusion, became self-righteous.

"I wanted to talk to you about Vinnie," I said crisply.

Marie's mouth tightened. Her hands, lying quietly against her thighs, now met in her lap and she twisted them together. "I knew it," she said, her voice soft with resignation.

"You *knew* it? How?"

"Come *on*," she said impatiently.

He'd like to see you," I went on.

"No," she said. "I won't."

"You won't? What do you mean you won't." This I had not considered. "Why not? He just wants to see you. To talk. That's all. He just wants to talk to you."

"There's nothing to talk about."

"How can you say that? There's everything to talk about."

"Not as far as I'm concerned."

"For God's sake. He's suffering. Doesn't that mean anything to you?"

"No. Why should it?"

"It's *you* he wants!"

"No, he doesn't."

"What do you mean, he doesn't?"

"He doesn't know me at all," she said. "How can he want me? It's not *me* he wants."

"Who is it then?" I was stupefied.

"Don't you know anything?" she said softly. "It's never *you* they want."

She looked down at her hands. I looked out at the pool. The sun climbed high in the late morning sky. I felt drowsy. A warm yellow fog filled my head. Years seemed to pass.

Marie looked up. I looked over at her. My head cleared instantly. It was true, I knew nothing, but the anxiety in that face! I saw how isolated she was, alone inside the words she had just spoken. Not one of us could have said what she had said, and she knew it. My heart went out to her.

"I won't see him," she said. "That's final."

My heart came back to me. Vinnie! Handsome Vinnie wouldn't get what he wanted and needed. I felt like slapping her. Who was *she* to deny *him.* She was nothing, no one, a name, a face, a body to which hunger had become attached. If I had put out my hand to touch her then I'm sure I would have felt glass, that's how unreal she was to me.

"Besides," she was saying brightly (she had just remembered something useful), "I couldn't. Even if I wanted to. There's somebody else."

"Somebody else?" My eyes shot open. "Where? In the city?"

"No. Here."

"Here? Who is it?"

"Eddie," she said.

"Who's Eddie?" I said.

"The bell captain."

"The *bell* captain?" I said and stared at her anew. The hierarchy of association was so strict in the mountains that if you were a waiter you had nothing to do with chambermaids or bellhops. (Marilyn's affair with the butcher was a matter of desperate dispensation.)

"Yes," she said, face flushed, head at a defiant tilt.

I didn't know what to do next.

"Is he nice?" I asked idiotically.

"No," the laugh was short and sharp. "But we understand each other," she said evenly.

I turned away from her and looked out again at the chemically colored water, the painted concrete, the striped deck chairs.

"It's all so disgusting," Marie said softly.

We rose without another word. I headed for the barracks, she headed for the side of the main building. For the first time I realized that she spent less time in the room between meals than any of the rest of us; Eddie lived just off the lobby.

That night Vinnie didn't see any of the people around him until he was crashing into them. I know he didn't remember any of his orders because his guests were yelling at him. Women who had loved him in the morning were now turning hurt, betrayed eyes on him as he forgot their special requests repeatedly and their husbands, feeling unmanned by the inability to control the quality of the service, threatened to become ugly. But Vinnie's gaze was fixed in space, his upper teeth nipping distractedly at his lower lip. No external threat could touch him. The next night he said he didn't feel well and would not be going to see Carol as usual. He spoke with exaggerated politeness: he knew he knew my name but for the moment it had escaped him.

Time seemed to expand and contract abnormally for days after that exchange, speeding up and slowing down for no discernable reason, as in a dream. In another minute the Labor Day weekend had arrived, and the season was about to end.

On Sunday, all day, the entire barracks seemed shrouded in a kind of convalescent inertness that contrasted strongly with the usual racketing-about that went on in our common hallway from six in the morning until midnight. The summer had, all at once, wound down with no resolution of the conflicts that had set the racket in motion. Abruptly, our agitation was ended. Now we were hanging on, waiting only to get sprung. The evening meal passed with less friendliness than ever before, many of us gone in spirit already. Faces were cool, guarded, remote. Vinnie's face, especially, was beyond reach.

Yet our bodies demonstrated a remarkable stylishness that night, arrived at with an energy fed, as never before, by the defensive cool. Trays were carried with the elegance of a dancer's control, the grace and skill of motion long ceremonialized. We were masters now, in possession of an art. Behind the seamless skill, well behind it, our sealed over young hearts.

At eleven o'clock that night Ricky and I sat on our beds, talking quietly, the room half pulled apart with our just begun packing. Outside our door hallway toilets flushed, sink faucets went on and off, rides were being arranged for. Suddenly, there was a muffled explosion against the wall behind our beds, and then everything was happening at once: the sound of furniture being flung, bodies thrown, a man's voice shouting, a woman's crying; waiters and waitresses running down the hall past the sinks nearly to the toilets, skidding to a stop, crowding into an open doorway, me and Ricky pushing forward with the rest; there inside, the chaos of cots half overturned, a bureau nearly pulled down, toilet things floating in the bedclothes as though on a shipwrecked sea, Vinnie in his black pants and sleeveless undershirt (muscles flexed, eyes glazed) and Marie, crouched in the far corner of the room, her uniform hanging in ripped shreds, clutching at her naked breasts, arms and neck covered with scratches already turning purple, her frizzy hair stringy with sweat, her crushed mouth twitching.

We stood there: cold with curiosity. No one looked at Vinnie. Everyone stared at Marie. She was in solitary. Waves of emotion came off her: hot and silent. It was her loneliness she was sending out. Her wise, humiliated loneliness. ("It's never you they want.") We looked at her out of our flat, young faces without pity or regret. She sat there, waiting. Her eyes flickered dully from one to another of us. They came to rest on me. I felt my own confusion—hard, mean, insistent—welling up.

"You asked for it," I said, and turned away.

But I have continued to look at her, for years and years. Her bony, knowing face still floats past me as she sits crouched in memory, forever trapped in that room with me, her keeper in the doorway, standing there upon a ground of brutish innocence that in more than thirty years has not given way, only shifted position many times over as I struggle ineptly to take in the meaning of her loneliness.

It was a world predicated on blind hunger: everything depended on the blindness. It took hard work to remain unknowing. Those of us who didn't manage it went into quarantine. Those of us who did required someone's humiliation at all times.

3 What feminism means to me

I'D BEEN SENT OUT BY THE VILLAGE VOICE to investigate "these women's libbers." It was November 1970. "What's that?" I said to my editor. A week later I was a convert.

In the first three days I met Ti-Grace Atkinson, Kate Millett, Shulamith Firestone; in the next three, Phyllis Chesler, Ellen Willis, Alix Kates Shulman. They were all talking at once, and I heard every word each of them spoke. Or, rather, it was that I heard them all saying the same thing because I came away from that week branded by a single thought. It was this: the idea that men by nature take their brains seriously, and women by nature do not, is a belief not a reality; it serves the culture; and from it our entire lives follow. Simple, really.

And surely this had already been said. How was it I seemed never to have heard it before? And why was I hearing it now?

It remains one of life's great mysteries—in politics as well as in love—readiness: that moment when the elements are sufficiently fused to galvanize inner change. If you are one who responds to the moment you can never really explain it, you can only describe what it felt like.

I had always known that life was not appetite and acquisition. In my earnest, angry, good-girl way I pursued "meaning." It was important to do work that mattered (that is, work of the mind or spirit) and to love a man who'd be an appropriate partner. These, I knew, were twin requirements: interwoven, one without the other unimaginable. Yet, I grew into a compulsive talker who could not bear solitude long enough to study. I did not learn to command steady thought. I read novels, daydreamed an important life, mooned over boys. Although I moralized endlessly about seriousness, it seemed I could pursue the man, not the work. This, however—and here we have something crucial—I didn't know. I did not know I could do love but I couldn't do work. I was always thinking, When things are right I will work. I never thought, How come I can still obsess over this boy or that even though things are not right?

In my mid-twenties I fell in love with and married an artist. I was all set. I had a desk to sit at, a partner to encourage me, a sufficiency of time and money. *Now* I would work. Wrong again. Ten years later I was wandering around New York, a divorced "girl" of thirty-five with an aggressive style who had written a couple of articles. Beneath the bluster the confusion was deep, the aimlessness profound. How did I get here? my head throbbed each day, and how do I get out? Questions for which I had no answers until I heard the "women's libbers." It seemed to me then that I saw things clearly. I was old enough, bored enough, exhausted and pained enough. The lifelong inability to take myself seriously as a worker: *this* was the central dilemma of a woman's existence.

Like Arthur Koestler getting Marxism for the first time, it was as though light and music were bursting across the top of my skull. The exhilaration I felt once I had the analysis! I woke up with it, danced through the day with it, fell asleep smiling with it. I became impervious: the slings and arrows of daily fortune could not make a dent in me. If I held onto what feminism had made me see I'd soon have myself. Once I had myself I'd have everything. Life felt good then. I had insight, and I had company. I stood in the middle of my own experience, turning and turning. In every direction I saw a roomful of women, also turning and turning.

That is a moment of joy, when a sufficiently large number of people are galvanized by a social explanation of how their lives have taken shape and are gathered together in the same place at the same time, speaking the same language, making the same analysis, meeting again and again in New York restaurants, lecture halls, and apartments for the pleasure of elaborating the insight and repeating the analysis. It is the joy of revolutionary politics, and it was ours. To be a feminist in the early seventies—bliss was it in that dawn to be alive. Not an I-love-you in the world could touch it. There was no other place to be, except with each other. We lived then, all of us, inside the loose embrace of feminism. I thought I would spend the rest of my life there.

What went hand in hand with the exhilaration was the quickly formed conviction that work was now something I could not do without. Loving a man, I vowed, would not again be primary. Perhaps, in fact, the two were incompatible. Love-as-I-had-always-known-it was something I might now have to do without. I approached this thought blithely, as though it would be the easiest thing in the world to accommodate. After all, I'd always been an uneasy belligerent, one of those women forever complaining that men were afraid of "women like me." I was no good at flirting, it was a relief to be done with it. If love between equals was impossible—and it looked as though it probably was—who needed it? I pressed myself against my newly hardened heart. The thrill and excitement of feminist reality made me glad to give up sentimentality, take pleasure in tough-mindedness. The only important thing, I told myself, was work. I must teach myself to work. If I worked, I'd have what I needed. I'd be a person in the world. What would it matter then that I was giving up "love"?

As it turned out: it mattered. More than I had ever dreamed it would. Yes, I could no longer live with men on the old terms.

Yes, I could settle for nothing less than grown-up affection. Yes, if that meant doing without I was prepared to do without. But the idea of love, if not the reality, was impossible to give up. As the years went on, I saw that romantic love was injected like dye into the nervous system of my emotions, laced through the entire fabric of longing, fantasy, and sentiment. It haunted the psyche, was an ache in the bones; so deeply embedded in the make-up of the spirit it hurt the eyes to look directly into its influence. It would be a cause of pain and conflict for the rest of my life. I love my hardened heart—I have loved it all these years—but the loss of romantic love can still tear at it.

It was always there, threatening, this split in me about love, yet I never spoke of it. I never spoke because I didn't need to speak. I didn't need to speak because it was bearable. It was bearable because I had made an important discovery. The discovery was my secret ingredient, the thing that made my cake rise each morning. It was this: as long as I had a roomful of feminists to come home to I had built-in company for life. I'd never be alone again. The feminists were my sword and my shield—my solace, my comfort, my excitement. If I had the feminists I'd have community, I could live without romantic love. And I was right: I could.

Then the unthinkable happened. Slowly, around 1980, feminist solidarity began to unravel. As the world had failed to change sufficiently to reflect our efforts, that which had separated all women before began to reassert itself now in us. The sense of connection began to erode. More and more we seemed to have less and less to say to one another. Personalities began to jar, conversations to bore, ideas to repeat themselves. Meetings became tiresome, parties less inviting.

At first, the change in atmosphere among us was only a glimmering suspicion (so solid had feminist comradeship seemed!), but slowly it became an unhappy conviction and then an undeniable reality. One day I woke up to realize the excitement, the longing, the expectation of community was over. Like romantic love, the discrepancy between desire and actuality was too large to overcome.

I fell into a painful depression. Existential loneliness ate at my heart, my beautifully hardened heart. A fear of lifelong solitude took hold of me.

Work, I said to myself. Work hard.

But I can't work hard, I answered myself. I've barely learned how to work steadily, I can't work hard at all.

Try, I replied. And try again. It's all you've got.

The first flash of feminist insight returned to me. Years before, feminism had made me see the value of work; now it was making me see it all over again with new eyes. A second conversion began to take place, the one in which knowledge deepens. I understood that I would have to face alone the very thing my politics had been preparing me for all along. I saw what visionary feminists had seen for two hundred years: that power over one's own life comes only through the steady command of one's own thought.

A sentiment easy enough to declare, the task of a lifetime to achieve.

I sat down at the desk, as though for the first time, to teach myself to stay with my thoughts: to order them, extend them, make them serve me. I failed.

Next day I sat down again. Again, I failed.

Three days later I crawled back to the desk and again I came away defeated. But the day after that the fog cleared out of my head: I solved a simple writing problem, one that had seemed intractable, and a stone rolled off my chest. I breathed easier. The air smelled sweet, the coffee strong, the day inviting.

The rhetoric of religious fervor began to evaporate in me, replaced by the reassuring pain of daily effort. I could not keep repeating "work is everything" like a mantra when clearly it *wasn't* everything. But sitting down to it every day became an act of enlightenment. Chekhov's words stared back at me: "Others made me a slave but I must squeeze the slave out of myself, drop by drop." I had tacked them up over the desk sometime in the early seventies, and my eyes had been glazing across them for more than ten years. Now, I read them again: really read them. It wasn't "work" that would save me, it was the miserable daily effort.

The daily effort became a kind of connection for me. The sense of connection was strengthening. Strength began to make me feel independent. Independence allowed me to think. When I thought I was less alone. I had myself for company. I had myself, period. I felt the power of renewed wisdom. From the Greeks to Chekhov to Elizabeth Cady Stanton: everyone who had ever cared to investigate the nature of human loneliness had seen that only one's own working mind breaks the solitude of the self.

A hard truth to look directly into. Too hard. And that is why we yearn for love, and for community. Both laudable things to want in a life—but not to yearn for. The yearning is a killer. The yearning makes one sentimental. Sentimentality makes one romanticize. The beauty of feminism, for me, was that it had made me prize hard truth over romance. It was the hard truth I was still after.

Everything I have just written: I have lost sight of times without number. Anxiety, boredom, depression: they overwhelm, they blot me out, I "forget." Slavery of the soul is a kind of amnesia: you cannot hold onto what you know; if you don't hold onto what you know you can't take in your own experience; if you don't take in experience there is no change. Without change the connection within oneself dies. As that is unbearable, life is an endlessness of "remembering" what I already know.

So where does that leave me? In perpetual struggle.

I have endured the loss of three salvation romances—the idea of love, the idea of community, the idea of work. With each loss I have found myself turning back to those first revelatory moments in November 1970. Early feminism remains, for me, the vital flash of clarifying insight. It redeems me from self-pity, bestows on me the incomparable gift of wanting to see things as they are.

I still struggle with love: I struggle to love both my hard heart and another human being at the same time—and with work: the daily effort remains excruciating. But when I make the effort I am resisting the romance. When I resist the romance—look steadily at as much hard truth as I can take in—I have more of myself. Feminism lives in me.

4 Tribute

RHODA MUNK DIED LAST WEEK, ALONE IN a car crash. The police think she pressed down on the gas when she should have used the brake. She was found behind the wheel, not a mark on her, staring calmly through the shattered windshield. I had known her twenty years, rejected and fought her in my head a good part of that time, turned my back often in her moment of need, but when I was told she was dead my arms and legs began to fill up with lead. I felt weighted to the earth. Something large, and wanting to be free, had gone out of the world. I saw that I had not known what she meant to me.

We met at a party a few months after *Woman and Authority* had been published. The book had come like lightning: a flash of excitement and danger that lit up the interior land-scape. It was the kind of writing that left you staring off into space with the book lying in your lap long after the last page had been turned. The framework was straightforwardly intel-lectual, but the flesh laid on those bare bones was the work of a poetic intelligence. The writer had used the daily experience of an ordinary woman to tell the story of authority and the hu-man race. The metaphor was startling. From the originality of Rhoda's juxtaposition the reader could see that woven into the apparatus of authority was, at one and the same time, the de-sire to grow up and the refusal to grow up; the longing to take one's place in the world, the resentment at having to take one's place in the world; the hunger for self-creation, the hatred of self-creation. The history of authority was laced through with the corruptions of prolonged infancy: exactly like any woman's life. It was a tale of self-division from start to finish: bitter and profound and told with the taste of iron in its mouth.

Many people found the book distasteful—the organization was a disaster, the tone off-putting, the line of thought diffi-cult to follow—yet the work compelled. The idea had a kind of genius that was instantly recognizable. A wide net had been cast, unevenly crocheted: some things fell right through the holes and the most amazing things fell into place, but the prose—dense, urgent, brilliant—kept dragging the deeps. Readers *felt* what they were thinking. For thousands, the book became an object of passionate devotion.

I had reviewed *Woman and Authority* in the *Times* with unstinting admiration and now, here before me at this party, stood the author of what I took to be a seminal piece of writing, a person who looked startlingly like the book she had written: a tall woman with elegant bone structure, rough skin, staring blue eyes (it was the eyes that nailed you), the hair a hank of wild brown straw glued to a lovely head: Vanessa Redgrave on a bad day: a natural beauty made coarse and interesting by the life with which it had been forced to associate. You felt that instantly with Rhoda: the way the parts refused to come together. You could see she was doing it to herself. She had a nervous habit of pushing the hair back repeatedly from the side of her face up into her temple. When she did that you became aware of her hand: the skin red and broken, the nails chipped and dirty, but the hand itself long, delicate, wonderfully formed. I was always so moved by those fine, raw hands. Later on, I wanted to catch them in mine, cover them with kisses, weep and press my cheek over them.

"I hope you're having fun," I said to her. "Everyone's talking about your book." The blue eyes opened wide and her face seemed to tremble. She looked at me so long I thought she was spacing out. Then I saw the mouth twitching, the shapely lips out of control. She hated my review, I thought. She's about to tell me it wasn't intelligent enough, I have failed to grasp the essence of her work, I have in fact done her a disservice.

"No one is doing a damned thing for the book!" she exploded. "Not the publisher, not the press, not the women. No one! You can't find it in the stores. I can't get my editor on the phone. People can't arrange for course adoption. It's terrible! Years of work going down the drain. An important book. . . ." Her voice trailed off and she was staring again. I looked at her in silence, amazed by the outburst, not even relieved to be off the hook. Whatever she's getting, I thought, it's not enough. It will never be enough. It's been too long in coming, too long by far. I was surprised by my own excitement.

I remember going to see Dr. F that first month, full of Rhoda, how mad and marvelous she was. Imagine. It had taken her twelve years to write *Woman,* but wasn't it wonderful? In the end she *had* written it, and it *was* a great work, and it *would* last, and . . . "Where are you?" the analyst cut in. "What is this all about?" "I don't know," I moaned dramatically. "Is it because she doesn't work *either?*" Dr. F demanded to know. "Is that it?" And of course that was exactly it.

I was thirty-five when we met, Rhoda was fifty. Most of my life I had wandered about, feeling locked out of my own mind. Love, fame, worldly adventure, all were as nothing next to the longing in me to sit down at the desk every morning and think: the one activity my conflicted psyche seemed bent on denying me. I had spent years on the couch railing weeping obsessing over what came between me and the desire to write. "I can't, I won't, I must, I can't" was the repetitive theme of my analytic complaint as I crippled on through. Now I had met Rhoda and I was excited. I *knew* what those twelve years were all about. I began to worship in her the incapacity I identified so strongly with. Here she was, brilliant, magnetic, and she couldn't do it either; only in Rhoda the condition seemed an exalted thing, moving and poetic: a statement, an analogue, a dramatic extremity. Anyone could see, a child could see, that in her the vitality was great and the depression bottomless. Sex, food, ideas, music, nature, politics, her eyes danced at the whole grand spectacle (and when they did anyone could catch her fire), but when Rhoda was in the room depressed oxygen left the air. She sucked the life out of a place with her bleak, stiff-necked, nostril-flaring silence. "I deserve better than this," the silence announced loudly. "Much better. And *you* are not giving me what I deserve."

What she had been—where she came from, how she made a living, how many husbands she'd had—did not signify. This was who she was, this repository of extremity, this largeness of anger and desire. Sex, her main appetite, was a paradigm. She raged at men like everyone else I knew, but she was hypnotized by them. She could never take her eyes off the men. She wanted to just want them, but she couldn't. She needed their recognition, and she needed their humiliation. "Look at that little ass," she'd say of some passing young man. "Couldn't you just bite into it like an apple?" Then one night, as we were driving uptown in the rain, she tried to run down some boys prancing across Third Avenue against the light. Her cheeks trembled as their startled faces loomed in the windshield. Her knuckles showed white on the wheel. "I hate the little fuckers," she hissed.

•   •   •

She had a way of being in the world that, from the very first, startled me, put me off then drew me back in, and when I came back I felt the strength of life anew. Ten days after we met we had dinner together in a restaurant on the Upper West Side. Later, I walked her home. It was early spring. In the doorway of her building she threw back her head, closed her eyes, and breathed deeply of the young night air. The eyelids quivered on her face and she kept her head held back for what seemed a very long time. The gesture was so prolonged I thought it affected. Then she opened her eyes, smiled directly into my face, and said passionately, "What a miracle it is, being alive." She was right, of course, it *was* a miracle. Why hadn't *I* remembered that? I was standing here smelling the same air as she. I felt the sweetness of the night then more strongly than I had in years and realized that she experienced the commonplace in such a way that in her company it was restored to me: I had more of the world than I'd had before.

We began to meet often, for coffee or dinner or an afternoon walk. Each time we met I felt again the impact of her eccentric beauty: the gaunt elegance, the penetrating blue eyes, the odd hungriness of the way she took in the world. She seemed to grow ever more animated, her insights richer and shrewder, her way of speaking expansive and more extended. The time we spent together—whatever it was, twenty minutes, two hours, an evening—began to have a shape we filled better each time we met. It wasn't only that I listened to Rhoda, it was that we listened to each other. I saw after a while that each of us was concentrated on what the other had to say. It was the concentration that was so striking: I'd never before been conscious of its presence in conversation. It made me sing inside. It wasn't that I came away thinking my words brilliant, it was only that I came away feeling I had been fully heard, and because I was being fully heard I was saying everything I had to say. It seemed to me, then, that ever since I could remember I'd been fighting for someone's undivided attention in conversation. Now I had it. I could breathe easy. I didn't have to be fast on my feet. I could think before I spoke.

Rhoda often had her head cocked as we spoke, as though she was hearing not only our own two voices but something beyond them as well, something she was calling to my attention. Look, her posture said to me, this is an ordinary thing we're doing, but just look at it. Two women listening to each other like this, recreating between them the meaning of conversation. It was another of her commonplaces. It gave me back more of myself than I'd had before.

Forgetting everything I already knew, Rhoda, I assumed, had *always* been heard. It didn't occur to me that being listened to was a live issue for her, but one memorable evening I learned otherwise.

Lena called and said she'd like to meet Rhoda, so would her husband, Johnny. They were a pair of lefties who were always feeling guilty about feminism; I found their efforts touching. "Sure," I said. "Tell you what, I'll make dinner and I'll invite Kayman as well." "Wonderful," Lena said. "I've been wanting to meet him for so long." We each got off the phone feeling we had something pleasurable to look forward to. Ten days later eight people sat down to dinner at my table: Lena and Johnny, Kayman and his wife, Carol, my neighbor Marilyn and her friend Toby, me and Rhoda.

Kayman is an old communist, a man who takes for granted that what he has to say will always be of central interest. His life has been formed by a conviction that everyone in the room is a student of his—they're either younger, more inexperienced, less intelligent, or else a woman or a child (the last two being categorically students). Men like Kayman had been dominating the table since time began: it was only natural that he would have expected the people at this dinner party to defer to him as well. But now there was another personality in the room as strong as his own. Everyone knew that *Woman and Authority* was being received as an intellectual event and that the beautiful exhausted-looking woman at the table was a contender, one whose moment had arrived. It seemed obvious to me that the evening was Rhoda's. It was her turn. Everyone could see that, no? As it turned out: no.

I hate to cook and hardly ever do it. When I invite people to dinner I'm not a guest at my own party until late in the evening. I don't even hear what people are saying until I've got the meal on the table. . . . So there they all were, Kayman sitting at one end, with Rhoda and Johnny on either side of him. Everyone talking talking talking, all I'm hearing is the buzz of New York dinner party chatter, I don't catch a word.

Then I'm putting the chicken and the green beans down and suddenly Rhoda is saying in a low clear voice that cuts through everyone's talk, "Why, you ugly little man. Don't you tell *me* not to interrupt."

Mouths hands voices: all stop at once. It is Johnny to whom she has spoken. Lena's face turns white. Kayman sits back in his chair, turns his body toward Rhoda, cocks his head and looks at her with real interest. Carol gazes down at the table and begins pushing her fork around in a circle. I'm so startled I nearly drop the food.

"For God's sake!" cries Toby.

"What is it?" I say. "What happened?"

Johnny stares murderously at Rhoda. "What happened?" he says to me, still staring at her. "She keeps interrupting Kayman. She doesn't let him get a sentence out."

Rhoda laughs bitterly. "That's a laugh," she says. She looks around the table, her blue eye cold and staring as on the first day I met her. "*Who*," she says evenly, "could ever stop *this* man from getting a sentence out. I thought I was helping things along, turning a monologue into a conversation. I didn't realize we had one man worshiping another here. That that was what was going on here."

Marilyn puts her head in her hands. "This sort of thing seems to be happening *constantly* lately. Can't we have a civilized exchange at the dinner table anymore?"

"That depends on what you mean by civilized," Rhoda says. "If civilized means one person at the table gets categorically ignored and is to remain silent about it then, no, I guess we can't have civilized exchange anymore."

"Jesus Christ," says Lena.

"Categorically ignored!" explodes Johnny. "I suppose that means *women*. Tell me something." He turns to the table at large. "Is this woman all women? Is that what she means? If she feels ignored, are all women being ignored? And why the hell does an interesting conversation have to be disrupted to go over all this bullshit yet one more time?"

"This bullshit," Rhoda bites off, her voice trembling with scorn. "What bullshit is *that* exactly? The bullshit that points out all the little murders of the soul that go on at the ordinary dinner party? Is that the bullshit you mean?"

"I think maybe she's got a point there," says Kayman slowly. "I think maybe she's right about that." The old Stalinist is the only person in the room with politics that go all the way down to the center.

"She is right," I say quietly. I want to say it hotly but I don't dare. I'm terrified of what is happening here. It's my dinner table, after all. The thought of people insulting each other at my own table, with me contributing to the insult, is dreadful. I can hardly take it in. . . .

I put all this in the present tense because I can still taste in my mouth the sickening dry excitement I felt that evening, the awful sense I had that the world as I knew it was cutting itself to pieces even as we spoke. That night I saw coming, as though for the first time, the death of sentimental affection between women and men. The familiar arrangement between

us was at an end. Our backing off, our silence, our turning the
other cheek: it was over. If Rhoda could not speak her piece at
dinner she'd have to leave the table. If she couldn't leave the
table she'd have to overturn it. Not one more time in her life
would she sit still to not be fully heard.

The next day, rushing about the city running errands, I
found myself cutting rapidly through Grand Central Station in
mid-afternoon. High up in a balcony alcove a gospel choir
from a church in Newark was singing Easter hymns: hosannas
for Bach and Western culture. I stopped to listen to the music. My body ached and I felt exhausted. Rhoda's glamorous,
ravaged face swam up before me: the twist of rage in her cold
blue eyes and the pain in her voice of scorn ("Don't tell *me* not
to interrupt, you ugly little man"). Suddenly, I began to weep.
A romantic sense of loss overcame me as I stood there in the
middle of the great train station, the tears streaming down my
still smooth cheeks. Rhoda's anguish pressed itself against my
heart. It felt large and grand and important. I knew I would
love it always.

"I've got a little house out on the island," she said one day late
in spring. "I'm going there next weekend to open it for the
summer. Would you like to come with me?"

"I'd love it," I said. I felt I'd been chosen.

"Good. Do you think you could me here at nine o'clock on
Saturday morning?"

"Of course," I said. "Any place you like." From the first it
had been any place you like.

On Saturday morning we climbed into her little red car and drove out of the city. The weather was glorious: soft and brilliant. Rhoda drove fast and well. Even when she was careless she seemed in control. Our conversation was like her driving: it went fast and well and even when it threatened to become reckless I was not afraid. I felt nothing could happen to me with Rhoda at the wheel.

Two hours later we were pulling off the road onto a narrow dirt path that began winding toward the sea. The path bounced over the ruts of an open field, moved into an enclosure of thickly planted trees, then on into the middle of a magical wood, wet and marshy, hung all about with ferns and mosses, gnarled roots and tender grasses. The tree closed, umbrellalike, over our heads for half a mile and more, and the road became a tunnel: densely woven and shot through with sunlight. Then the trees separated and we burst onto a grassy green bluff that plunged straight down to a stony beach and the open waters beyond. There, filling our eyes our lungs our hearts, was the silvery sea, shining in the warm spring sun. I had been brought to a place of bright living beauty.

On the bluff stood Rhoda's house: an old-fashioned camp cottage, brown shingled and built low to the ground, the kitchen doorstep settled into the grassy earth, the wall beside it covered in thin black vines that in a month or two, I knew, would turn green and bear a wilderness of flowers. The entire house was enclosed in plywood shutters. We got out of the car and Rhoda unlocked the front door.

A large central room dominated the cottage, with a screened-in sleeping porch off to one side and another porch, half enclosed, facing toward the sea. Beyond the central room were three small bedrooms separated by thin partitions, a tiny kitchen with windows all around (one of them cracked), and a rude bathroom with a jammed back door and a rusting water heater. In the kitchen a broken plate was heaped in shards on the counter and a paper shade on a wall light had a hole burned through it.

Rhoda walked through the large room to the porch facing the sea. She found a long stick lying on the low wooden enclosure and with it propped open one the shutters: a small square of sea-colored brightness burst into the room. She propped up one shutter after another, making of them a row of wooden awnings that framed the room in shaded light. On the porch stood a table and some chairs. I sat down in one of the chairs and then the world, at eye level, became a little composition of grassy bluff, silvery sea, blue blue sky. Joy filled my heart: unshadowed and primary colored. I thought: I could sit at this table forever. I want to sit at this table forever. And when I leave it I want to leave it only to walk with Rhoda on that stony beach down there, talking of women, men, and the world as we find it.

The place was Rhoda's creation. We had traveled across field, wood, and marsh, through tangled growth and shaded enclosure, to arrive at a house that was shabby and beautiful and civilized the landscape. Without the house the world was a glorious emptiness, with the house I was seated in the middle of created space. The space imposed coherence: inside this house one could listen and one could think. From here, I felt, I would go forward.

Rhoda invited me to share the cottage at the seashore that very first summer; said she'd work better with a friend like me in the house. The invitation made me happy. I *had* been chosen. I began to daydream our walking on the beach by the hour, talking on and on in a conversation without closure. Her mind would roam freely in my company, my own would expand to take in the richness of hers. I would give her the telling response she rarely met with, she would give me the mentorship I still craved. A glorious summer lay ahead.

We went out to the beach in June. Bring what you like, Rhoda had said, invite whom you like. Wonderful, I'd said, and thought no more about it. I would take what I always took—one suitcase and a bagful of books—and invite no one. Whom did I need or want to see? Not a soul. I was there to be there with Rhoda: to concentrate on the exchange, make a drama out of listening. Surely, she wanted the same. Wasn't that, after all, the thing between us? our great enterprise? the reason she had invited me?

The first week was one of those astonishing moments in life when exactly what you've fantasized materializes: Rhoda and I, cocooned together in the tumbledown cottage, settling in happily to talk and to work: I at a book I'd been hacking away at for two or three years and Rhoda readying herself for the second part of a projected trilogy, of which *Woman and Authority* had been the first. This next volume was going to matter even more than *Woman* had. It was the book that would make clear the largeness of her concerns, the scope of her vision. She had been thinking about it for a couple of years. Her ideas were not formed but neither were they inchoate. She was on the verge. Any minute, we both knew, she was about to begin. I felt honored that she saw in me a beneficent presence on which to calm her spirit and gather her thought.

Our first days together passed in a contented rhythm of shared solitude. In the mornings we each went to our separate places (hers on the sleeping porch, mine in one of the small bedrooms) to sit with our work. At one o'clock we met for lunch. After lunch we separated to read. The afternoon sea glimmered through the screened porches and the cats prowled freely, roaming across our laps at will. Rhoda's cats: she had a passion for these animals, there were four of them at the cottage. She loved them, she said, because they were beautiful and they knew it: they had no need to earn existence. She would stare at them by the hour, as though if she looked long enough they'd tell her something she needed to know.

Late in the afternoon we'd throw the cats down and go to the beach where we walked, read, skimmed stones at the ocean, and swam about not far from shore. Swimming was a religion with Rhoda. She walked into the water every morning and every evening, ritually. At those time she would stand on the beach in a long cotton gown and wide-brimmed straw hat, looking out at the horizon, a peculiar sort of stillness seeming to gather in her. Slowly she would disrobe, cross to the water's edge, wade in, and here too she would stand for a long motionless moment. Then she'd plunge, lifting her lovely arms one at a time in a high arcing motion, striking out for the distance, quickly achieving a rhythm that was incantatory, unmistakably incantatory. She was communing with the sea: reestablishing herself in the natural world. But in the afternoon, when I joined her, it was only us larking about in the water together—splashing and calling out to each other, laughing to hear our voices split the air—our pleasure an extension of friendship. At seven we walked back to the cottage and made dinner. At midnight I went to bed calm and happy. In the morning I awoke warm and expectant. Peace began leaking into me.

On Friday afternoon—without warning or announcement—her friend Karen arrived. "Oh," said Rhoda vaguely. "Didn't I tell you she was coming?" A few hours later Rhoda's nephew Mark arrived, and in the morning her student secretary, Carrie. None of these arrivals was accompanied by a word of explanation. Rhoda's manner was serene and impassive, somehow beyond question. We five spent the weekend together. Mark and Carrie played Monopoly, Karen knitted, I read, Rhoda cooked—and cooked and cooked.

The kitchen, it had turned out, was the important room in the house. It was here that Rhoda had had the most to unpack when we arrived. From bag after bag she had removed, slowly and carefully, implements and utensils made of plastic, wood, and aluminum; gadgets made of stone, wire, and bakelite; cups and plates in ceramic and woven straw; jars and pots in glass, copper, and china. There were boxes of food as well, string bags and canisters filled with tea and foreign spices and homemade mayonnaise. Rhoda, it seemed, loved nothing better than to roll up her sleeves and prepare an elaborate meal, making thoughtful use of half the items in the kitchen. Cooking, she said, was a way to make art and give love. She worked steadily that first day, humming contentedly to herself as she put all this stuff in its place—on shelves and hooks and wires strung from the ceiling—and in no time at all the kitchen was a roomful of cheerful clutter: bright and busy. Too bright, I thought once or twice, much too busy. My eyes became distressed when I let the whole room invade my senses at once. Rhoda too seemed to space out in the visual noise. She'd stand sometimes at the counter looking all around her for something she needed—let's see now, where is that cup, strainer, garlic press? Then I'd see her find her way *in* and retrieve what she needed. A great smile would light up her face. It gave her pleasure to perform this exercise. Sometimes her pleasure was so great it was almost as though the clutter had been created that she might perform the exercise.

The meals, of course, were (literally) fabulous and imposed a rough coherence on a group of people who, on the face of it, had no reason to be sitting down together: each person at the table turned like an eager puppy toward Rhoda when she spoke and away like a bored old dog when anyone else spoke. But the company *did* have something in common and slowly, as the weekend progressed, that thing stood revealed. They had all known Rhoda for years, and every one of them had spent the first summer of friendship at the cottage.

By Sunday morning the meals had become a burden. We, none of us, seemed able to remember why we were there. I was so depressed I began to feel unreal to myself. In distress, I turned to the sea for comfort, but the loveliness itself had become an abstraction.

A stream of people began trickling in from that second weekend on; a stream that never ebbed, never flagged, never slowed down or dried up. They came in twos and threes, ones and fours. They were young they were old; they were women and men; white, brown, and yellow; they were students neighbors cousins; acquaintances of a moment, friends of a lifetime; ex-sisters-in-law and discarded lovers; teaching colleagues and fans of *Woman and Authority*. Impending arrivals were never announced, invitations never discussed. People simply appeared.

Rhoda occupied the kitchen as though on a mission, often complaining that she had no time to work. When I urged her to go to her study, telling her we could prepare the meals ourselves, she would look frantic; as though she had, somehow, been overtaken. No, no, she'd exclaim. She couldn't do that. These people were her *guests*, she couldn't leave guests to fend for themselves.

Bewilderment rose like the tide twice a day in my unhappy chest, bewilderment and a miserable sense of inadequacy. I must have gotten it all wrong, from the very beginning. It now seemed to me that not only did Rhoda not want my companionship but was actually avoiding it. People were being invited to make sure that she would never have to be alone with me. And, after all, why not? Who was I? How could I have hoped to hold her interest? Clearly, I was insufficient. Yet, whenever we *were* alone—for a morning, an afternoon, even a day or two—she seemed as happy as ever to spend the hours in my company roaming the beach together, our good talk a steady flow, our quiet moments easy and natural. I could not puzzle it out.

One evening, after a long day filled with the aimless chatter of the usual six ill-assorted people, I walked down to the beach with her for her ritual swim. She moved carefully over the stones to the water's edge, I beside her but not looking at her. Neither of us spoke. The evening was cool and bright, heartbreakingly soft. Then I turned to her. I saw her face in the fading light. She stood there at the water's edge looking out at the horizon. Behind her were the people, ahead of her the natural world. The expression on her face was one of intense relief. It was the intensity that did it. Suddenly I thought, She's in solitary. It isn't that she loves nature, it's that nature helps her forget how alone she is when she's with people.

I saw then: it wasn't that she didn't like me, she liked me very well, but it didn't matter how much she liked me, or anyone else; or what she talked about with me, or with anyone else. Soon, quite soon, she'd be feeling alone again: emptied out. No one she knew could fill her up. If she swallowed all of us at once she'd still be hungry. She required constant replacements. Some of those replacements might be more talented, more interesting or entertaining, than others but in the end we'd all have to be replaced. None of us could accomplish the task for which we had been asked to come.

I'll never know whether Rhoda felt my withdrawal and she herself withdrew in response, or if her increasing remoteness was preordained by what I thought I'd learned of her that evening at the shore, but by Labor Day the honeymoon of our friendship was over. Never again after that summer did I imagine myself Rhoda's special intimate. For all intents and purposes, I joined the motley company at the weekend table.

And company it definitely was: composed of people who'd each been drawn to Rhoda, each felt special for a time, then each fallen swiftly out of closeness, yet remained attached to the idea if not the reality of the connection. We'd get together sometimes, those of us who'd met through Rhoda, and we'd talk, inevitably, about her.

At these meetings I began to distinguish myself. Everyone knew that Rhoda was depressed. I alone insisted she was in the grip of lifelong rage. "The depression is really rage," I said, and kept on saying it. Sometimes when I spoke, an eye glinted, a brow was raised, a head nodded in vigorous agreement, but no one concentrated on the equation as I did.

"Yes, yes," would come the response, "but listen to this. The other night she was saying, really she *is* brilliant, the way she puts things together . . . "

I pretended to listen. I was waiting for the moment in the anecdote when I could pounce. Inevitably, I'd find it and announce triumphantly, "That's really the rage speaking."

I could deliver whole monologues on the subject of Rhoda's rage, and deliver them I did. I had had a compelling insight, and I would not let go of it. In the company of those who knew her my insight flowered into compulsion. Sometimes it was as though I'd gone into a trance, so mesmerized had I become by the beauty of my own single-minded interpretation.

People became impatient with my one note analysis, even irritated. Why? I always wondered. After all, I was only supplying the corrective. Wasn't that obvious? Everyone here had come to worship. I alone saw what no one else saw, understood something no one else understood. How could I not speak? Why was this not appreciated?

The years passed. Rhoda and I continued to meet, less often and usually without satisfaction. I felt her drifting in my company. She had wanted from me, I told myself, either deference or salvation, and since I could provide neither . . . I'd shrug then inside and, while we were still together, turn back into myself as we walked or talked or ate a meal. Yet, whenever we actually agreed to meet it was always with expectancy.

Meanwhile, the lifelong struggle to work proceeded apace, going on and on—and on. Like my relationship with Rhoda, it never got resolved, never got abandoned. Somehow, I crippled on through, perpetually waiting for the clouds to lift so that I could write a review, finish an essay, develop a book.

And everyone waited for Rhoda to complete the sequel to *Woman and Authority,* which, of course, no one ever doubted she would. This second book of hers was the Holy Grail toward which we were all traveling. "When Rhoda's book gets written . . . " became a refrain among the people I knew. It meant: we will then be in the presence of visionary clarity; all will be understood, and all forgiven.

More years passed.

Then Rhoda took a trip to India and came home with a new husband. She was now fifty-eight years old, the man she married was forty: a car mechanic from a hilltop village, a handsome brown-skinned person with liquid eyes who wore the turban of the Sikh, spoke singsong English, and appeared clever but desperately confused to find himself waking up in a New York City apartment. You could see in his face that he was constantly wondering where the sky had gone, how it was that the mountains and valleys of the earth had disappeared. He thought Rhoda had placed him under a spell. He would grin at the visitor and announce, "I wor-r-ship her." Whenever Selim said "I wor-r-ship her" I would think, One of these days they'll find her murdered. But Rhoda only laughed and stretched herself contentedly. I can still see her at sixty, two years into Selim, waking up in the morning, in that mess of a bed on the sleeping porch with the cats all over her, her body half exposed, her face smoothed out, beautiful, and filled absolutely filled with sexual pleasure: a creature out of Colette. The marriage lasted four years.

In the second summer that Selim was with her Rhoda invited me to spend ten days with her at the cottage. On the first Saturday Andrea, a former student of Rhoda's, arrived for the weekend. This Andrea—a small woman with flashing eyes and a mass of dark hair she was forever tossing back—was a psychologist at the city university. It was said she was making a career for herself, but the only way I ever knew her was frantic over some new infatuation she herself was unconsciously sabotaging. Rhoda was intensely fond of Andrea: she reminded her of her own young self.

Now Andrea was pacing the large front room of the cottage at midnight, after a late dinner Rhoda had taken a full two hours to prepare, telling us about Jason who, three months into their affair, was already becoming disaffected. They'd gone camping the previous weekend. Jason was a big wilderness man, Andrea knew nothing about life outdoors. While he prepared the campsite for the night she sat on a tree stump reading aloud to him from the *New York Review*. (I laughed. Andrea looked at me. "Something wrong with that?" "No, no," I shook my head, "go on"). The piece she was reading had excited her. "Listen to this," she had said to him, thinking she was being comradely. But he had turned away in the middle of a sentence. When she protested he said curtly, "What's the difference? You only want someone there while you're performing."

"Omigod," I said.

"Yes!" Andrea leaned toward me, her eyebrows arched dramatically. "And I saw what he meant!" She tossed her hair. "I knew he was right." She held the hair away from her face with delicate fingers. "It didn't used to be this way," she moaned.

"No?" I inquired.

"No! In the beginning he read my stuff, he liked what he read, he's smart, he was incisive. Now . . . " she moaned again. "I've been too critical. That's what he says. He says, 'You find all the soft spots, the weak spots, and you lay on the scourge of your critical tongue. You've picked and picked and picked at me.' He loved me! I've destroyed it."

I stared at the floor. Andrea buried her face in her hands. Rhoda looked out toward the kitchen where Selim was washing the dinner dishes. It was taking him hours to clean up, and I knew why. The kitchen was even more cluttered than I remembered—more teapots, more baskets, more egg timers— it had been mesmerizing to watch Rhoda find her way ever more slowly into the visual noise she herself kept increasing. Now Selim stood at the sink, juggling desperately to put a washed pot or dish down on the crowded counter, his movements trapped in a web of necessary caution.

"I don't like male energy," Rhoda said thoughtfully, peering at the kitchen. "Too hard, too forward, too direct. The gestures, the motions, the whole repertoire. Too limited. Not like with women. No nuance, no modulation. It's not attractive. And then sometimes it's suffocating . . ." She stopped suddenly, as though she'd come to a thought she couldn't complete. She looked off into some invisible middle distance in her mind. Then she sat up in her chair, shook her head, ran her hand through her disheveled hair and laughed. "When I was young," she said to Andrea, "men were the main course, now they are only a condiment. I advise you to arrive at that same state as soon as possible. Life is do-able only then."

This isn't true, I thought, it can't be true. She is wanting Andrea to conclude that men mean little or nothing to her but I know better. Yet, what *did* they mean? When she spoke of love as the main course she was, I knew, remembering a time when she hungered for men who refused to give her terms; when she spoke of love as the condiment she really meant making a man need her whom she didn't need. No doubt men remained linked up to old angers but could it be that she was still involved at this simple level of sexual power seeking? Was it for this—either he gets humiliated or I do—that she had brought Selim back from India? Was that the hidden motive behind such extremity? This was hard to believe.

One morning toward the end of my stay at the cottage I was awakened by the sound of Rhoda's voice in the kitchen—loud, hysterical, grief stricken—calling out to Selim, "How could you! How could you! Are you so *stupid?* Or are you trying to kill me? Is that it? Have I taken you into my house and my life and my bed so that you can put an end to me? Is that why I have brought you here?" I leaped out of bed and ran toward her voice.

Rhoda stood in the middle of the kitchen in an old worn out nightgown, tearing her hair. Her eyes were haggard, her mouth quivering with unhappiness. Across the room, facing her, stood Selim, his hands spread against the wall, his eyes wild. The room looked like a tornado had hit it: stuff everywhere, pulled off the shelves, out of the bins, down from the counters. Between Rhoda's legs stood two creased shopping bags (one with a large grease stain on it), overflowing with scraps of waste paper. Selim, it turned out, had been cleaning up, had found the bags at the back of a curtained alcove and had just been about to throw them out. The scraps of waste paper were Rhoda's notes for the still unwritten second book. If a full bladder hadn't pulled her out of sleep, and an errant thought hadn't sent her looking for part of an old note. . . . She'd pulled the kitchen apart looking for the bags. "You you you," she screamed at Selim, her voice shaking with rage: her unslaked rage, her beloved rage.

I looked around me at the chaos in the kitchen, the chaos in the shopping bags, the chaos in her voice. At the end of the chaos was the unwritten book. Now I understood what Selim was doing here. Selim did not know who in the world she was. Only a man who did not know who she was would do what he had done. What she needed to *have* done. She had gone to the end of the earth to bring back the man who would secure her chaos. Because no doubt about it: it was still a man who was the required instrument of her own undoing.

I stood in the kitchen watching them, and suddenly I was remembering the first time I had seen the cottage and how I had thought then, From this place I will go forward. The memory was iron in my mouth.

After that summer I did not see Rhoda for two years.

When we met again Selim had gone back to India and she had still not begun to write her second book. One day I walked into her kitchen in New York and realized she never would. The disorder in the room had passed into another dimension. Every surface was crowded with an alarming indiscriminateness; juicers and shredders, coasters and keys, pills and cat food, anchovy paste and felt-tipped pens, crackers and eye drops, timing gadgets, warming gloves, message pads. There weren't two square inches of space for the eye to rest on. My heart began to beat fast. Rhoda stood at the sink with a paring knife in one hand, a potato in the other, talking eagerly to me as she worked. She turned once to look at me. When she turned back to the sink she stopped moving. Her body looked puzzled. "Where's the knife?" she asked. I stared at her. "In your hand," I said slowly. "Oh," she said, and laughed. She shook her head as though to clear it. Two minutes later I saw that she was losing her concentration again. This time she was too canny to give herself away. She stared into the sink until she forced herself to remember where the knife was. She is driving herself into senility, I thought calmly. She would rather go senile than give up the rage.

When I left her my heart was beating even faster.

At the funeral a crowd of people spoke: students, colleagues, lovers; readers, fans, swimming companions; friends of childhood and the friends of maturity. No two stories were alike yet only a few themes emerged. The repetitions were vivid, the variations absorbing. Women seemed to speak exclusively of her "powerful eros," men of her "penetrating intellect"; and each group displayed a kind of bad-tempered contempt for what the other one knew.

Beside me sat the woman who'd replaced me at the cottage the summer after mine. "Do you hear what I'm hearing?" she whispered. I nodded at her. "This is so exactly what Rhoda spent her life looking at." Then she said, "She was like Keats, all she did was observe what was around her." I turned in my seat, to stare at my companion. It seemed a thousand years since I'd had such a thought about Rhoda. The woman got up to speak.

"It was in conversation with Rhoda," she said, "that I changed from a smart girl into a thinking person. With her the line of insight began to draw itself out of me. My stride length-ened, my grasp was extended."

A student of Rhoda's got up. "She taught me how to listen to the conversation in my head," he said. "From her I learned that the struggle would be to talk to myself."

Another student spoke. "She was always surprising us. We went to see *Platoon* with her one night. We all hated it and went on and on about the movie glorifying war. 'I liked it,' Rhoda said. 'Wha-a-t!' we all yelled at her. She beamed at us. 'Have you ever *seen* such a wonderful depiction of the miser-able obedience of men?' she said. We would never have thought of that ourselves."

"She had two stories she told over and over again," said a friend of thirty years. "Parables, she never tired of them. In one a woman falls off an ocean liner. Hours later, she's missed. The crew turns the ship around and they go back. They find her because she's still swimming. In the other a young man decides to kill himself, jumps off a high bridge, changes his mind in the air, straightens his body out into a dive, and survives. Rhoda would always find an opportunity and start telling one of them as though I'd never heard it before. Sometimes it was as if *she'd* never heard it before. That probably says more about her life than anything else. The despair, the boredom, the loneliness. It all translated for her into, The species is doomed, it will destroy itself, but ya gotta keep swimming."

Bullshit, I started to say to myself, rage was the sea she floated in, the water she never . . .

Suddenly the words died in me. The familiar thought refused to complete itself. I saw that it was myself I was talking about. It had always been myself I was talking about. I had never really known Rhoda, never seen her whole. I had used her as I needed to use her.

She is my melancholy, I thought, my inner divide, my downward pull, the thing I have understood least. It has pleased me to spend the years nailing down Rhoda's rage, as though by spotting it in her I would diminish it in myself. With her, I had indeed come to worship incapacity. That way I could remain devoted to what I most hated in myself.

I stared across the room at Rhoda's casket . . . the years of good talk I had sent to the bottom, the gold sunk, the dross retrieved. . . . I stood up in my seat. Someone was speaking. All eyes were on me. What could I do? The ship was hours gone, and I such an inexperienced swimmer. I turned and walked toward the open door.

5 at the university: little murders of the soul

THE OTHER NIGHT AT A PARTY IN NEW YORK I ran into Charlotte; next day in a restaurant I saw Daniel; the day after that in the post office Myra. I have loved these people—how I have loved them!—and all for the same reason. I am hungry for the sentence structure in their heads. It's the conversation between us that makes me love them. Responding to the shape of their sentences, my own grow full and free: thought becomes expressive, emotions clarify, and I am happy, happier than at any other time. Nothing makes me feel more alive, and in the world, than the sound of my own mind working in the presence of one that's responsive. Talking with Charlotte or Myra or Daniel the grittiness washes out. Connected to myself, I am now connected to others. Solitude is relieved. I am at peace inside my skin.

Yet in each case I could not hold onto the friendship. I failed to comfort as well as stimulate. With me *they* did not clarify. In my company each became more fragile, more complicated, more self-involved, not less. I did not give them back themselves as they wished and needed to have themselves returned. In friendship as in love peace is required as well as excitement. Unless both are present, the graft does not take. Connection remains a matter of the unreliable moment. Without steady connection the friendship has no future. In New York anything without a future is instantly flung back into the distracting surge.

Failure of connection among like-minded people is a preoccupation of mine. The people I know are all talkers: people for whom conversation is vital, the kind of people who if they're not talking don't know they're alive. Yet, many is the evening I have sat in my chair after a gathering of some sort staring into the emptiness of the past few hours, thinking about the words spoken among "people like ourselves"; words that should have opened us to ourselves but had in fact shut us down, left us feeling abstract and demoralized. Which, I wonder as I sit alone late at night, was the sentence offered as a stimulation but received as a challenge; the nuance that put Daniel off rather than drew him in; the response that scattered Charlotte's insight and flattened Myra's spirit? Why did it happen so easily, and so often? Why did we come so close, yet remain apart? Everyone in the room was decent, intelligent, literate. We all pulled the same lever in the voting booth, read the same book reviews in the *Times*. None of us was in real estate or city government. What had gone wrong here? The answer was always the same.

Good conversation is dependent on a simple but mysterious fit of mind and spirit that cannot be achieved, it just occurs. It's not a matter of mutual interests or class concerns or commonly held ideals, it's a matter of temperament; the thing that makes someone respond instinctively with an appreciative "I know just what you mean," rather than a challenging "What do you mean by that?" In the presence of shared temperament conversation almost never loses its free, unguarded flow. In its absence one is always walking on eggshells. Shared temperament is analogous to the way a set of gears works. The idea is not complicated but the mesh must be perfect. Not approximate, perfect. Otherwise the gears refuse to turn.

It's years of university teaching that have made me think about temperament. In university towns one sees countless "people like ourselves" living whole lives inside the isolation of what I've come to call the Syndrome of the Approximate Response, acclimating daily to the repeated sound of the phrase, the nuance, the sentence spoken by a colleague or a neighbor that makes one shrivel rather than expand. It is a kind of death in life to which university people become inured.

I once worked in a writing program in the South where another writer working with me was a woman my own age from New York. This department also boasted a Black Mountain poet as well as a novelist who wrote magic realism and a philosophic nature essayist. Before I left New York people said to me, "What a golden company you are fallen among. You're in for a winter of great conversation." As it turned out, none of us had very much to say to one another. The woman from New York was religious, the magic realist an alcoholic, the poet pathological on feminism, the nature writer socially autistic. By which I mean, Who knows what any of them was really like? Not I. All *I* know is that in their company I felt abstract, and in mine they felt the same.

The New York writer and I were both Jewish and we'd both been to Israel. One night at a dinner party she and I were explaining the country to the others.

"In Israel you can heal yourself of modern life," she said.

"Only in Tel Aviv do you feel like you're in the world," I said.

"The country brings you back to original values," she said.

"You feel like you're choking on nineteenth-century politics," I said.

"There you recover the power and beauty of the family," she said.

"The sexual immaturity is unbelievable," I said.

Every time I opened my mouth I heard in her response, "What do you mean by that?" as she did in mine.

We were temperamentally mismatched, all of us. We remained a collection of expatriates, isolated from one another, each of us hanging there in solitary southern space.

It was a period of exile not because of the inability to connect but because I was unable to talk about the inability to connect. Whenever I raised the matter my colleagues looked at me: first puzzled, then uneasy, then dismissive. I was making a great deal out of not very much, I was told.

"Who needs all that socializing," the magic realist said.

"It's a relief to be left alone," the essayist said.

"I don't know what you're talking about," the poet said.

I've been teaching on and off for more than ten years now. I go out, I come back, go out and come back. These stints of mine are only a matter of three or four months—I couldn't leave New York for any real length of time—but there are more hours in four months than I could ever before have imagined. It isn't just that a weekend can last three years in a university town; after all, that can happen anywhere. In New York a good depression easily slows the raging hurry down to a dreamy sleep-walk, any day of the week. But in the city no matter how dragged out the day, the hours remain, somehow, grounded. A limit is placed on the *idea* of isolation. I may not be making love myself but the air I breath is charged; I am not doing politics, it is true, but there is politics in the daily exchange; my own appetite is without edge yet appetite is clearly the coin of the realm. When the hours grow long in a university town I walk streets that are empty of people, silent and motionless. The dreaminess thickens. Soon, there are no human reminders. I start to free-float. Sunny tree-lined streets become a moon walk.

It's the silence, especially, that gets to me. As the days and the weeks accumulate it deepens: sinks down into flesh, presses on bone, induces a pressure in the ears that comes back up buzzing. It's a silence created in streets where sex and politics die early because conversation is not a daily requirement; expressive language has passed out of common usage; people speak to transmit information, not to connect.

Mine has been a pilgrim's progress through the university. I have passed back and forth among the provincial, the respected, and the patrician where I have sometimes been welcomed, sometimes ignored, sometimes received with the civility accorded an equal. Each encounter has had its consequence. Embraced, I learned one thing, shunted aside another. But, inevitably and in all cases, I am struck by the open space into which daily exchange falls, the buzzing silence that surrounds the earnest chatter. The history of that silence is what I've learned about at school.

Stirling, Maine, was a movie-set college town: white frame houses, hundreds of maple trees, lawns enclosed by low stone walls. Some neighborhoods were good, others better. The marginals were literally at the margin: you had to drive to the edge of town to see peeling paint and trashed front yards. From any house that an academic might be living in the world spread out in all directions: safe, gentle, prosperous. There were women on the faculty, blacks on the campus, and divorce in abundance, but a deep settled conservatism governed the atmosphere: one of working husbands, mothering wives, the politics of the world an abstraction.

I was the only visitor in the writing program that year, and nothing about me was designed to promote easy friendships among the permanent faculty—I was a woman, a New Yorker, a writer who lived primarily off her writing; they were men who had spent many years in Stirling, writers who wrote sparsely if at all, and lived academic lives—but as it turned out they were a somewhat boozy lot, eager to welcome the stranger in their midst. Every Friday afternoon the writers gathered at four o'clock in a friendly hotel bar just off campus, and one of them always stopped by my office to say, "Coming, kid?"

The words were part of a style they had all adopted. The style was an anachronism—heavy drinking, tough-guy locutions, ironic weariness—one that belonged in a World War II movie, not on an American college campus in the eighties, but it was a way these men had of separating themselves from the place in which they lived. They came together, I soon realized, on these Friday afternoons to rage like expatriates against their outcast state. I had never before heard people speak with so reckless and impassioned a contempt for the circumstance in which they passed their lives. The sentence structure of scorn grew ever more resourceful as the writers reviled themselves, and each other, for spending their lives teaching the unteachable.

One man in the writing program was made conspicuous by his absence on Friday afternoons, a novelist named Gordon Cole. Apparently, Gordon and Stanley Malin—a writer always in attendance on Friday afternoon—did not speak to each other, hadn't spoken in years. Where Gordon went Stanley failed to appear, and where Stanley presided Gordon was sure to do the same.

The disagreement between the two men had originally to do with what courses to assign writing students. Stanley had said students of writing should study everything, poetry, fiction, and nonfiction. Gordon had said nonsense. Why did a budding novelist have to waste his time learning how write an essay he was never going to write? After some years the men had quarreled violently over this philosophic difference; such an impasse had been reached that now they were unable to speak or even sit easily together in a group of their colleagues.

The quarrel, its depth and insistence, was puzzling to me, as I was repeatedly struck by how well matched these two seemed in intelligence, breadth of outlook, and literary ardor. What a pity, I often thought, that each was denied the pleasure of the other's mind. No one else in the program spoke of books and writing as freely, as vividly, as did both Gordon and Stanley, no one relished thinking out loud as much as they. Having coffee with one or the other, the entertaining high-mindedness of the conversation inevitably warmed me through and through. Yet neither could do for the other what each one so easily did for me. For each man the sentences the other spoke had become an infliction—and then a wound. Mention one to the other, and the face of the man in front of you instantly formed itself into a mask. Behind the mask neither man could be reached.

Stanley Malin was a teacher of writing in a style I remembered: an old-fashioned curmudgeon. Writing was holy and he made the girls cry. Brilliant, naive, arrogant, he might stand before a class and intone, "The writer must rend his flesh. He must lay himself open to the pain. The suffering. The reader must *feel* the crucial rending of the flesh." Then suddenly he'd drop the rhetoric and announce in a voice blunt with authority, "Good writing has two characteristics. It's alive on the page and the reader is persuaded that the writer is on a voyage of discovery." When Stanley spoke in this voice anyone could learn from him.

But is was not only the girls Stanley made cry. After thirty years in Stirling he'd done that to almost everyone who had crossed his path. His mind was made in the shape of a steel trap. He had a way of encouraging people to open up quickly —the interest was penetrating, he asked many questions, one flourished in a matter of minutes—then he'd find the weak spot in the work, the argument, the personality, and he'd close in. Just as quickly, one would be made to feel a fool. You'd talked on and on, and you'd hung yourself.

His was the seductive power of an original mind coupled with a spirit of such startling negativism that people were drawn to the pleasure of his sentence structure only to find themselves wounded by the malice of his observations, and then amazed to be coming back for more. Eventually, of course, they turned away from that belittling tongue, that scorning clever mind, that excoriating need to take everyone down. Sooner or later, all men and most women walked away from Stanley feeling themselves the sum of their disabilities, and then they sought him out no more.

He was alone, and only slowly did I understand that he could do nothing to remedy his isolation. Behind the brilliant derisiveness lay a passivity of monumental proportion. Stanley Malin was a man who if the light went out in the room he remained in the dark; if he walked out in the morning and found the car had a flat tire, he turned around and went back in the house for the day; if a woman said she was leaving him unless he spoke more intimately with her, he told her to make sure the door was closed on her way out. All Stanley could do was wait for people like me to come through town. Everyone else had been used up.

Gordon Cole was as sociable as Stanley was reclusive. His wife had people to dinner once a month, and when a visiting writer or intellectual was in town she routinely produced an evening for eight or ten. These dinners had been going on for twenty years. There were one or two couples who were always in attendance, and five or six others who showed up at every second or third party. Nearly every man in the room was in the English department, and nearly every woman in the room was a faculty wife. The company ranged in age from forty to sixty and the conversation was, with rare exception, what is called civilized. Strong opinion was unwelcome at the table, and sustained exchange was experienced as tiresome.

I discovered that people introduced subjects in order to

allude, not to discuss. There'd be three minutes on the head-
lines, seven on European travel, two on Friday night's concert.
Real estate often went a good ten or fifteen minutes, and so
did taxes and the cost of schooling for the children. Books
never came up, and neither did the students.

Gordon was a puzzle to me at these dinners. Immensely
considerate of his guests—pulling out chairs, passing dishes,
refreshing drinks—his manner was uniformly affectionate.
He'd sit smiling amiably when someone at the table began an
anecdote full of promise, continue smiling long after it had
become apparent that the point being made was too simple to
be interesting, and I would see that his smile was fixed. He
had stopped listening halfway through the story. His was the
attentiveness of the genuinely detached. In one sense he welcomed people to his house, in another he was more of a
stranger in the room than I.

Above the mantelpiece in the Cole living room stood a
row of leatherbound Balzacs. Once, I began leafing through
Cousin Bette and found myself moved by the beautifully worn
pages, the absorptive thought in the marginalia. The book itself was an act of love. This was the Gordon with whom I
talked when we were alone at school, a man for whom literature remained alive and life-giving. But here at the party this
Gordon disappeared and in his place was a man of impenetrable politeness. Watching his masked face at the table I often wondered where he was at that moment, and in whose
company. One night I realized that he was nowhere, and with

no one. Gordon Cole at his own dinner table was the equivalent of Stanley Malin slumped in the dark, sitting beside a phone that no longer rang.

In time the two men became emblematic to me. In my mind's eye I saw each of them sitting alone, encircled by an isolation that spread through the silent streets across the town, out to the margin, to the peeling paint and the trashed yards neither of them ever had to look at. A tide of emotional bewilderment would rise in me. Here they were, thrown together in this small tight world, each one longing for the kind of conversation the other could supply, yet each one locked into insult and injury less than a mile apart. At that moment, the littleness of life seemed insupportable, its impact large and its consequence inevitable.

A week before I left Stirling a history teacher named Barsamian was arrested. He'd been caught slashing the tires of another history teacher, a man named Wallerstein. The incident was reported in the local paper. The memorable detail in the report was that Barsamian and Wallerstein had had a falling out (over standards) fifteen years before. The two men hadn't spoken in years.

I remember staring at the sentence, the one about them not having spoken in years. I remember thinking, Wallerstein has remained alive in Barsamian's brooding mind all this time; alive and central; an instrument of inflamed injury felt each day as they pass each other in the department corridor, sit in the same room for a committee meeting, brush past a table in the faculty club.

I was accustomed to the murderous pathologies of New York, but this was different. This was Chekhovian. These people felt violated in their souls by an atmosphere that denied them sympathetic understanding, and the violation had come to fill the inner landscape. Again bewilderment rose in me. It was inconceivable to me that intelligent, decent people should reduce themselves to eccentricity. Why was this happening?

These thoughts separated me from the people with whom I taught at Stirling, turned me into a narrator and them into characters. When I said good-bye I felt I was on one side of a human divide, they on the other. I was made of different stuff. What was in them could never be in me.

The situation was indeed Chekhovian. My turn—like that of the doctor in *Ward Six* who understands confinement only when he himself is at last imprisoned—lay just ahead.

At Stirling they hadn't known Derrida from an insurance agent. At the University of the Farwest they not only knew who Derrida was, they knew the name of his publisher and the size of his last advance. Stirling was time warp: a place where everything important had occurred years ago, and people were now living with the outcome of lives long decided. At Farwest nothing was settled and no one had made peace. The department quivered with restless ambition.

Eight men and one woman taught writing here. They were novelists and poets in their mid or late fifties, many of whom had achieved a moment of fame during the sixties. I soon discovered that each of them held the place they found themselves in at a discount. One and all thought they belonged somewhere better. The atmosphere reeked of brooding courtesies and subterranean tensions. I did not for a long time understand exactly what it was I was looking at. I had never before encountered mass depression.

A graduate student picked me up at the airport on a Friday afternoon and drove to the dormitory rooms that had been secured for me. I arranged the stark little apartment to suit minimal needs and then went out for a walk. The town was calm, spacious, western, the streets wide as boulevards, the mountains cut out against the sky. Once again: houses and trees, no people. All as silent and motionless as it had been in Stirling, but here the clarity of the light and the sweetness of the air were so powerful they became a presence. It was Monday morning before I realized that, except for a few phone calls from home, I'd not spoken to a human being the entire weekend.

One by one, the following encounters took place in the course of the week:

A tall fat man stood beaming in the open doorway of my room. "My name is Dennis Mullman," he said. "I've written nineteen books and they all hate me." I laughed, and he asked how I was getting on. I told him I didn't know as I hadn't yet met anyone. "That's how they are here," he said bitterly. "No one's interested in anyone. They're all wrapped up in their own miserable selves." He withdrew, promising to be in touch soon.

"I'm Lewis Waldman," said a voice in my ear as I stood at the secretary's desk in the English office. "Oh, hel-lo," I turned enthusiastically to face a boyish-looking man dressed in blue jeans and a tweed jacket. I recognized the name as that of the program director. "Let me know if you need anything." He waved the pipe in his hand at me and walked away.

A woman darted at me in the mailroom. "Hello hello hello," she said in a loud friendly voice. "I'm Sabina Morris. Am I glad to see *you!* Gotta get together. Talk about *Noo Yawk*. Can you buh-*lieve* this place? Twelve years I'm stuck here. Just think about *that* for a minnit." She rolled her eyes to the ceiling. "Lissen, we gotta get together." I nodded and said I had nothing but free time. "Nah," she said, pushing the air away with her hand. "Famous writer like you?" She snapped her fingers. "You'll be all booked up in a minnit. Lissen, I'll call you. We'll get together."

A cherubic-looking man—red-cheeked and gray-bearded, wearing blue jeans, sneakers, and a moth-eaten sweater—came toward me on the street. When he got close enough I saw the anxiety in his bright blue eyes. "Hi," he said. "I'm Sonny Coleman." He was one of the three New York novelists I knew had spent the last twenty years at Farwest. "How ya doin?" "Okay," I said hesitantly. He laughed. "Well, one good thing about this place. They leave you alone." He saluted me good-naturedly and went on his way.

A week passed, two, then three. I met my classes and walked the streets of the town. The air and the light still felt like company but on Friday afternoon of the fourth weekend I left a note in Lewis Waldman's mailbox. "I'm beginning to feel like a trespasser rather than a visitor." I wrote. "What's up?" Sunday morning, late, my phone rang. "Jeez," Waldman said. "Your note took me by surprise. I thought you were meeting people all over the place." No, I said cheerfully, that wasn't the case and since this was the fourth weekend in a row I hadn't seen anyone or gone anywhere, I thought I'd let him know. "Well," he said, "how about dinner tonight with Irwin Stoner and the woman he lives with?" Wonderful, I said, and hung up thinking, Now everything will be all right.

At seven o'clock sharp Waldman arrived in his tweed jacket and blue jeans and we drove off to a basement restaurant in an old hotel that here too served as a university meeting place. A handsome couple rose in their seats as we entered the room. The woman was tall with a headful of curly blond hair, the man of medium height with a delicate face and gray-brown hair cut so that a thick strand of it kept falling over one eye. We all shook hands and sat down.

Irwin Stoner was the writing program's Famous Person. He had written six novels in twenty-five years, all published in counterculture presses. The first three had been applauded, the second three reviewed respectfully. He'd been teaching at Farwest for years. I had looked forward to meeting him.

In the weeks that followed I tried to retrace the course that evening had taken, to see if there'd been a specific point at which we could have done it differently, but I was never able to locate the moment; and in fact I don't think there was one. We had simply been ourselves. With every set of observations made, and responses received, the distance between us had cracked wider.

"What a relief it must be to get out of New York," Stoner said.

"Not, really," I said. "It's just that I can't make a living in the city."

"It's great here. They leave you alone," Waldman said.

"I hate being left alone," I said.

"How can you write with the literary Mafia breathing down your neck?"

"I live below Fourteenth Street. The Mafia doesn't leave midtown."

"You see that establishment shit getting published all the time, it's demoralizing."

"Everything get published nowadays, not just establishment writing."

"How can you say that! Christ, if you're any good at all you can't *possibly* get a decent reading in a mainstream house."

"Are you kidding?" I said. "Never before in the history of the world has so much writing gone to print, good and bad alike."

"What are you talking about! Susan Sontag has a stranglehold on the intellectual press. Without her say-so nothing gets accepted."

"You don't really believe that, do you?"

Abigail Duffy, the Spanish teacher who lived with Stoner, laid a restraining hand on his arm—"Please, Irwin," she kept saying, *"please"*—but he shook it off. His skin was now flushed, his eyes sparking. He leaned into the provocation. I saw that my presence, certainly my perspective, was acting like an electric prod on him, making him cry out in lively anguish, putting the color back in newly angry cheeks. The thought made me lonely. My mouth closed in mid-retort. When it opened again it was to say, "Perhaps you've got a point there." I grew conciliatory, and the argument ground to a halt. After that, we worked hard to repair the torn-up atmosphere but in no time, it seemed, we were all out on the street inhaling gratefully into the cold night air.

Irwin Stoner was in advance of all that was to come.

Do what I would I could not make connection at Farwest. I had competed successfully, it seemed, for the right to visit among people none of whom wanted to know me. I had coffee, lunch, a chat at the mailbox with each person in the department, once. No disasters, no repeats. The exchanges were pleasant, even amiable, and always left me feeling abstract.

I tried to hear myself as I might have been heard, but I could not. I'd run into a writer or a teacher in the corridor or on the campus, we'd stop to chat, I'd be asked how I was and I'd answer—in three full paragraphs, as someone once said of me. Maybe it was those three paragraphs. I had always considered the fullness of my reply the only generosity I know myself to possess. But at Farwest, where people replied in one sentence, I saw eyes glaze over as I launched into the third paragraph. Those glazed eyes sank me. They cut me adrift. Once adrift, I was lost. I could learn nothing, about myself or anyone around me.

I taught my classes, read, went for long walks, sat at my desk, and spoke nearly every day with someone in New York. Yet, increasingly, I became more and more aware of those around me with whom I did *not:* talk or walk or eat. "Why doesn't *he* want to know me?" I'd find myself thinking as I collected my mail. "Why doesn't *she* want to have coffee?" walking across the campus. "Why don't *they* invite me to dinner?" in the middle of reading a student paper. The faces of my indifferent colleagues appeared in the air before me, occupying not my thoughts but a space on a field of inner vision. Gradually, these faces appeared so often they made the space shimmer, and then the field itself expanded to accommodate my unhappy concern. New York receded in imagination. My friends became voices on the telephone. Every day now the people who did not speak to me loomed larger than those who did. I began to brood.

The absence of response became a presence in my life. Out of this presence came a sense of isolation that grew steadily more pervasive. Inside the pervasiveness a vacuum formed. Inside the vacuum I began to feel not merely alone, but under quarantine: a human substance to be avoided. Possessed of an acute need to make connection I became, more than I had known myself to be, a creature of immediate experience. I was losing an inner balance whose precariousness took me by surprise.

A woman who taught seventeenth-century lit became symbolic of the rejecting world. She's one of the best, I'd been told, gracious and scholarly, an asset to literature and women's studies, a person I'd surely want to know. Friendly enough when we met, thereafter in my presence this woman did not speak. If she passed me in the hall she averted her gaze. If I walked into the lounge and she was reading a newspaper she'd glance briefly at me and, without a word or a nod, return to her paper. If she was forced to look into my face she'd manage a brief wintry smile. She had about her an air of aloofness that radiated judgment. It was a kind of behavior I had long ago shut the door on, but now at Farwest it began to invade me. Each morning when I awoke this woman's face flashed in the air before me, and angry distress flooded my heart. Once, years before, at a writers' colony a young poet who'd been feeling miserably left out of things had fantasized me at the center of a clique that was deliberately excluding her. The seventeenth-century lit teacher would have been amazed to learn that she had now become to me what I had been to the poet.

The classroom could only reflect my troubled state. The students were grave, blond, silent. I heard my voice growing thin and rhetorical. I must have said "profound," "original," and "important" fifty times an hour about books whose originality and importance would have been self-evident had I not been performing in a void.

I called a friend in New York, the wisest and most talented teacher I knew.

"They just stare at me," I told her. "I talk, and they stare."

"Darling," Ann said, "they *want* to speak, but they don't know how. It's hard for them. *Adults* don't know how. You know that. People like you and me, who are asked a question about a book, or anything else for that matter, and marshal a full response in a matter of seconds, we're rare. And these are *children*. For them it's sheer terror. They want to respond, they want to please you. They've read the book. They have feelings. But they can't find a way in to save their lives. They sit there with that puzzled frowning look on their faces. . . . The teacher who finds the questions to let them speak is setting them free for the rest of their lives. Releasing them into an articulateness their *parents* don't possess."

"Omigod," I moaned. "I can't do this."

Ann laughed straight into the receiver. "It takes years," she said. "Years."

I hung up and sat staring at the phone. A light came on in my head. I will go to the students, I thought. I will say to them, On the other side of your silence is a suffering human being. They will understand, and they will act.

Then the face of the woman who taught seventeenth-century lit intervened between me and my bright thought, and the flare of hope dimmed. If *she* could look at me week after week without a word or a nod why should *they* speak to me?

At a university reception I stood facing a scientist and a historian with a glass in my hand. The scientist was old and European, his voice resonant with the sound of one at his ease in the drawing rooms of the world, an adept at educated small talk. The historian nodded in all the appropriate places, supplying his own share of anecdotal banality. The men turned to me, inviting me to add, subtract, do what I will. I opened my mouth to speak, and nothing came out. Suddenly, I had not a thing in the world to say. At that moment I could not imagine that I had ever had anything to say, that any words of mine had ever animated an exchange, improved a conversation, given pleasure. I looked blankly into the face of each man. Then I excused myself, and walked away.

We all know that we are interesting only relatively speaking; but we don't really know it; and secretly we believe otherwise. To be faced daily with the suspicion that actually you may not be interesting *at all* is a frightening circumstance to negotiate. First you think, It must be them, it can't be me. Then you think, No, it's not them, it *is* me. Getting to the third thought, It's not them, it's not me, it's the two of us together—that takes some diving. At Farwest I shuttled back and forth between the first two, never even approaching the third.

One day, weeks after the reception, I ran into the European scientist. He asked me how things were going.

"All right," I said, perhaps ten seconds too slowly.

The scientist shifted his books from one hand to the other, adjusted his glasses, and looked at me.

"One thing you got to know about academics," he said. "Either you're too good for them, or they're too good for you."

It was my turn to look at him. I had nothing to shift of to adjust. The moment extended itself.

"You mean I'm too famous for the timid and not famous enough for the ambitious."

"You got it," he said.

"But surely the world isn't divided between the timid and the ambitious."

He made no reply. Instead he raised his hand to an invisible hat brim, saluted me, and went on his way.

I stood looking after him. Something broke loose inside, and there flared up in me a bitter torch of anger. Unjust! I cried to myself. Unjust.

Sabina Morris came hurrying down a path destined to cross mine. She was always hurrying. Once or twice a week since I'd been here she had rushed past me, halloo-ing, "Gotta get together." Today, sure enough, she called out, "I'll phone you, we'll have lunch." I put my hand out and stopped her. "Listen," I said, "it's okay to just say hello. We don't have to go through this charade whenever we run into each other." Instantly she cried out, "Do you know what it means to *live* here! You fancy visitors come out, you think all we got to do is entertain you. I work *constantly*. If I'm not teaching I'm grading papers. If I'm not grading papers I'm at committee meetings. I have no *life* here, no life at all! You don't understand! Nobody understands! We get no understanding at all!" And she rushed off.

Two days later the scientist invited me to dinner. His wife was a psychologist in the town. I told her of my encounter with Sabina Morris.

"She really believes that," the psychologist said, "that she has no time. But what it means is that she can't do anything because she has to recover every day from what it feels like to be talking *all the time* to people with whom she only rarely engages—the students, the colleagues, the deans. That's why *most* academics have no time. Only they don't know it. It's the not knowing that makes them so unhappy.

"If they knew *who* they were, and *where* they were, they'd take the bad with the good with more equanimity, and life would then be infinitely more cheerful. But as it is, they live in a continuous state of worried anxiety because this is not what they signed on for. What they signed on for was a 'life of the mind.' . . . Nobody thinks any of this out before they go plunging after tenure. . . . They all come to the university with a fantasy of intellectual gifts they expect to have nourished. But most of them, it turns out, are neither thinkers nor scholars, they're simply hardworking teachers. This, it seems, is an impossible reality to adjust to. It *feels* as though recognition of the talent within is being withheld—by all these nasty, inferior people all around them. Sabina Morris will spend the rest of her years here being eaten alive over the wrongness of her life and hating, absolutely *hating*, the students, her chairman, the provost, the chancellor. It's all because of *them*."

I found myself relishing the psychologist's words. It made me happy to see it her way, to think Sabina Morris passive and cowardly, a dream-ridden woman made small and ungenerous by self-deception. It's because *she* can neither absorb nor rise above her circumstance that things are as they are here, I thought. If *she* was different life here would be different. If *she* had more vitality, more experience, more detachment *I* would not be feeling trapped in a tight mean world. Smoldering, I realized for a moment, as much as she. But I let the moment go. The thought of Sabina Morris's moral and psychological deficiencies was giving me too much pleasure. The righteousness of my own pain burned in me, and I held the burning dear. In fact, I drew closer to the fire.

That night I lay on the couch in my sublet apartment, hands locked behind my head, gazing up at the empty square of white ceiling. I saw that I was in the grip of a humiliation I was inflicting on myself, yet I felt powerless to bring it under control. No, not powerless, unwilling. It pressed like a tumor against the inner wall of a fully fleshed chest I now thought of as narrow and bony. I needed the humiliation to fill myself in.

At midnight I understood why Barsamian had slashed Wallerstein's tires.

Impala U. is one of the richest schools in the country, and its writing program one of the best. The faculty publishes steadily and lives at the end of a continuous flow of invitations to readings, conferences, symposia. Sitting in the middle of the California desert, the university sparkles with green grass, stone fountains, red-tiled roofs, and palm trees. No one teaching here wishes to be somewhere else. Everyone knows this is the place to be.

At Impala there were weekly lunches, monthly readings, picnics and galas, museum openings and film festivals. The wives of doctors and lawyers had been put on a board of trustees that gave them access to the writers; they, in turn, raised money for student fellowships. The faculty was amused by the arrangement and fell in easily with organized events, as well as casual meetings around school that included students, staff, and townsfolk. A loose-knit camaraderie prevailed that sounded a note of light-hearted civility. We're secure enough, it said, to be accommodating.

Mack Dienstag, the friendly language poet who directed the program, found me an apartment, showed me around town, and gave an entertaining welcome dinner. At the dinner were Lloyd Levine and Paul Braun, a pair of poets in their late thirties; Kermit Kinnell, the program's Famous Novelist; and Carol Riceman, a critic-essayist in her forties. These people seemed to enjoy one another. Soon the banter among them picked up speed, and then direction. Within minutes it had equipped itself with a line of thought, making each of us sound intelligent in our own ears. What a good time I was having! I could not know that, for the people at the table, this dinner was obligatory. The months ahead looked promising.

The apartment was comfortable, the schedule easy, and the generic character of social life in Impala suited me well enough. I might take in a movie with one of the writers, but just as often it might be a doctor's wife or a graduate student inviting me to dinner: equally pleasing. What, after all, did I care where I got invited, or by whom, so long as I wasn't sitting home alone night after night as I had at Farwest? Yet I did remember the pleasure of that first evening and puzzled sometimes over why it failed to replicate itself.

I saw the people who'd been at the table almost every day, but in some crucial sense I didn't see them at all. Now and then I'd walk into Lloyd Levine's office to say, "Let's get together." "Definitely," he'd always reply. "This week is bad, we've got so many visitors coming, but next week for sure. Anyway, I'll see you at the department lunch on Tuesday, and at that reception on Friday afternoon. We can talk then." A day later I'd have the same exchange with Mack Dienstag or Carol Riceman and walk away feeling expectant but uneasy. The talk at lunch would inevitably be of writing program business and at the reception it was dinner party chit-chat: three minutes on the local art opening, seven on London versus New York, six on the fool in the White House. I was always left feeling tired, wanting only to get away. Meeting up with Mack or Carol or Lloyd at one of these affairs was, in a way, worse than not seeing them at all.

It was at Impala that I came to realize: when people find themselves in spirit-diluting proximity three times in a single week they have no urge to search each other out for an evening of real conversation. The memory of negative feeling lingers in the nerves and is aroused for a good twenty-four hours after by the sight of those with whom you've committed the emptiness. At none of these affairs did anyone ever suggest getting together afterward. Neither, I noticed, was the suggestion made if any of us ran into each other the next day at school. Compulsive socializing, I began to see, stirred up dissatisfactions that weren't allowed to clear out, they just kept on buzzing. Proximity was a hornet's nest.

One afternoon Sarabeth Kinnell called to say they had a visitor from New York, why didn't I come over for a drink. I was on my way to Mack Dienstag's to pick up a book I'd left at his house but sure, I said, I'd stop by. Later on at Mack's, I mentioned in passing that I'd just been at the Kinnells's. "Oh?" he said. "Are they having people over?" Something in his voice sounded a warning. Not really, I said, it had just been a spur-of-the-moment invite.

"Who was there?" he asked, carefully.

Why? I bantered, had he wanted to get out of the house?

"No," Mack said. "I hardly *ever* want to leave the house. I *love* being home." He hesitated. Then he said, "I just can't stand being left out."

"You're kidding?" I said.

"No," he laughed. "I'm not."

"What do you mean, left out?"

"It's crazy, I know. It sounds crazy even to me, but there it is. Mostly, I find gatherings a bore. I'd rather be home reading. But when I think the others are getting together, for whatever reason, and I'm not invited, I can't stand it. It preys on my mind."

"Which others?"

Mack smiled a broad, heavy smile. "The ones that count, he said, smiling ironically."

"I don't get it," I plowed on. "If you really want to stay home what does it matter who's getting together with whom? And if you *don't* want to stay home, what's the difference where you go as long as you have somewhere to go? Like Keats said, any set of people is as good as any other."

"You really believe that?" Mack said. "That any set of people is as good as any other?"

"Absolutely," I said firmly.

He sighed and handed me my book.

"You don't understand what it's like here," he said. "And it's hard for me to explain."

I found these words remarkable. At Farwest I had brooded over not being invited to dinner by people I didn't like, but here at Impala, where the company was plentiful if not ideal, I thought, What an ingrate you have to be to become neurotic over who is, or is not, inviting you to dinner. I should have known by now that to separate myself so grandly from a fellow sufferer was a guarantee I'd soon be eating my own distinction.

Impala dinner parties were, at first, a relief and a comfort. The amiability had so strong an effect on me that I was surprised my colleagues didn't feel as I felt at almost every table. I'd mention something interesting I had heard at the Dixons's, and Mack would say, "Oh, do you see them?" "Yes," I'd reply, "don't you?" "I used to," he'd say. "Used to see a lot of them. But haven't for years now." "What happened?" I'd ask. "I don't know, exactly," he'd say. "I guess we just ran out. . . . " This was a sentence I heard repeatedly. "We just ran out." Rarely, if ever, did I hear of a friendship ripening at Impala; almost always it was a tale of exhausted spirits having been arrived at.

It amused me, to hear them speak so, and then one evening—at the Dixons's, actually—the amusement suddenly evaporated. It struck me that almost every sentence I spoke that contained a piece of my mind had to be negotiated. The path leading to unimpeded thought was never clear, always clogged and strewn about with the ubiquitous "What do you mean by that?" So many exchanges seemed to bog down at the introductory stage, making the journey to a point obscure and wearying, most wearying. Why had I not seen this before? And why did I now seem to see nothing else?

It was at Impala that I first isolated the Syndrome of the Approximate Response. At the time I thought only that it was being inflicted on me. Then one night I delivered the Approximate Response myself, on a mildly grand scale, and the dynamic came clear. Things fell into place. I understood why the auditoriums during public readings grew emptier and emptier as the term progressed. I also understood why Mack Dienstag was preoccupied with being left out.

A famous Israeli poet came to read. He was handsome, self-contained, remote; a courteous smile played on his lips but he glazed over visibly when others talked. Paul Braun didn't show up at the dinner before the reading, and neither did Mack or Kermit. Serena and Lloyd Levine came, Carol and her husband, and me. Lloyd performed nonstop. He knew the poet's work by heart and had come prepared to give him the educated admiration every writer wants. The poet accepted Lloyd's deference benignly, while giving almost nothing back.

As we got up from the table Serena Levine said to me, "Isn't he sweet?" I looked at her. "No," I said, "he's not. He knows who he is at all times." Serena's eyes rested lightly on my face. "Believe me," she said, "for a man who knows who he is at all times he's sweet." I gazed at her in admiration. She *had* put in her time.

Then the poet read. From his cold mouth there issued images of beauty and of power. Throughout the reading I felt repeatedly what I had often felt here before: the extraordinary up-welling of a large spirit housed in a man of ordinary dimension. He spoke a great deal, much too much for a poet, his speech edging always toward pontification. Then he'd read a poem. Out would pour some stunning economy of insight and tenderness, and you'd be his all over again. The performance exhilarated and discomforted.

Afterward there was a reception, to which hardly anyone came. Faculty hurried away, and so did the students. None wished to submit themselves to the Great Man. Lloyd seemed exhausted, and Carol got frantic, insisting we all come back to her house for a drink. She couldn't bear for the poet to return to New York thinking Impala boring and provincial. In her living room he settled heavily into his chair, his face impassive, his eyes hooded, no longer benign. You could see, he had sung for his supper, he'd had it with the small talk, he wanted out, now.

Lloyd slumped on a couch across the room, staring at his shoes. He too had sung for his supper; he no longer knew what to do. The atmosphere infected me. I felt I had to entertain the company. I sat down on a hassock halfway between Lloyd and the poet, turning adeptly back and forth between them, and began to speak—brightly, quickly, fluently—about a trip I'd made to Israel. The poet sat back, a finger ridging his temple, his boiled eyes watching me, giving me no help at all. I spoke of Josef Brenner, saying the poet's work reminded me of Brenner's complicated feeling for Jerusalem. I explained Brenner to the others, a brilliant, early modern Hebrew novelist, little known in this country, just being rediscovered. I came to the end of my speech and turned like a good girl to the poet. He stared at me so long I thought he'd lost his English. Then he spoke.

"Actually," he said, a finger still in his temple, "Brenner's work is nothing like mine. Nothing at all. There is no resemblance whatever between us. And he is not brilliant. In fact, he is dull, quite dull. He is not being 'rediscovered.' He's been around all the time. We don't pay attention to him because we know how dull he is. But Americans come, and they make a fuss over him. They *discover* him. . . . " He shrugged and stopped talking.

The blood had left Carol's face and Lloyd was looking wild. I wanted to throw back my head and laugh out loud. The poet felt as I did when some brightly stupid person makes the same kind of sloppy-comparison mistake with me, and I'm not in the mood for a rescue mission. He wanted what I wanted: conversation that would nourish. Instead, he was getting junk food, empty calories. And so were we. I glanced over at Lloyd. His face had collapsed in weariness. None of us was getting what we needed. I saw then why the academics stop coming to these things: a sufficient number of such exchanges and the death of the heart threatens.

I also saw what led, paradoxically, to the obsession with being left out. When the meal is unsatisfactory often enough you become hooked on the idea that somewhere else people *must* be eating well. In a small, tight world, somewhere else inevitably becomes the people to your left and to your right who sat down last night at a table you were not invited to.

I found myself pitying the people around me. And then, of course, it was my turn.

One Tuesday, as the writing faculty was scattering after its weekly lunch, I heard Lloyd say, "Carol, sorry about that Proustian thing last night." "What Proustian thing?" Paul asked. Lloyd turned to him. "Remember when I called the waiter over and said to him . . . " I didn't hear the rest of the sentence. My mind had clouded over. They had dinner together, I was thinking, the three of them, they didn't invite me. They get together all the time, they never invite me. For the rest of the walk back to our offices I talked but I heard nothing: not what I said, not what anyone else said.

In the evening I lay on the couch with a book in my hands. I'd turn a page and on the page it would say, "Lloyd and Carol and Paul have dinner together all the time, they never invite me." The phone rang twice—my agent called from New York to say the book was doing well in England and a doctor's wife called to invite me to dinner. Each time I hung up, happy for a moment. Then the anxiety returned: Lloyd and Carol and Paul have dinner together, they never invite me.

I got up to make a cup of coffee. This is ri-*dic*-ulous, I said sternly to the pot of nearly boiling water. But the admonishment did no good. The brooding went on, for hours and for days. Whatever I was doing—teaching, reading, driving—suddenly I would remember "Lloyd and Carol and Paul," and the thought was a needle in my heart. All I wanted was: *their* company, *their* attention, *their* fun. Everything else was the booby prize.

That weekend a writer I knew well came to visit, and we spent a wonderful evening together. I heard my sentences being received exactly as I sent them out. Because the ones I spoke were being responded to, I had more of them to speak. Because I had more to say I felt myself filling up. At the end of the evening I left the restaurant well fed. The hour was late. The heat had died down. I walked for a while, breathing deeply into the clear desert air. For the first time I realized that nowhere in Impala did I have the conversation that gave me back myself. I didn't need much of it, one in fact would do, but I did not have that one. I had many approximations, but not the thing itself. Hence the brooding over Lloyd-and-Carol-and-Paul.

I felt acutely the difference between the city and the small tight world. In New York if I feel bad about not being invited somewhere, the phone will ring shortly and I'm invited somewhere else just as good as the place I'm not being invited to (there, any one of six conversations will do). The brooding is a matter of minutes or an hour. I clear out quickly. I remain open, fluid, uncalculating. Here, at the university, the pain lingers. I cannot clear out. It is hard to heal. Because it is hard to heal I must defend myself: close off, grow scar tissue, thicken my hide. Speech becomes guarded. I give up expressiveness.

Or else turn into a lunatic.

I saw that I was losing it. I had thought as much, and then one day I was told as much. Serena Levine took me to lunch to let me know I was experienced as *violently* critical of: Impala, the university, the writing program. They were all, she said, beginning to feel alienated from me. My words were taken as a judgment on their lives. "You think you're only speaking your mind," she said bitterly, "but you're like the foreigner who takes you into his confidence while he trashes your country." On and on she went. I replied hotly. And then we each stopped talking at the same moment. The sun climbed high in the noon hour sky. The haze thickened and burned. Serena stared down at her plate. I looked out into the middle distance. University buildings began to shimmer. The silence between us accumulated. Here we sat, a lonely writer and an insecure faculty wife, each being made neurotic by isolation of the spirit induced at an institution in service to the life of the mind. The silence buzzed in my head. The heat became unbearable.

Marriage promises intimacy; when it fails to deliver the bond is destroyed.

Community promises friendship; when it fails to deliver the enterprise is dissolved.

The life of the mind promises conversation; when it fails to deliver its disciples grow eccentric.

It's easier actually to *be* alone than to be in the presence of that which arouses the need but fails to address it. For then we are in the presence of an absence and that, somehow, is not to be borne. The absence reminds us, in the worst way, that we are indeed alone: it suppresses fantasy, chokes off hope. The liveliness we start out with is stifled. We become demoralized and grow inert. The inertness is a kind of silence. The silence becomes an emptiness. One cannot really live with emptiness. The pressure is terrible; unendurable, in fact; not to be borne. Either one breaks out, or one becomes inured. To become inured is to fall into grief.

6 on living alone

IT'S SUNDAY MORNING, AND I'M WALKING UP Columbus Avenue. Couples are coming at me on all sides. They fill the street from building line to pavement edge. Some are clasped together looking raptly into each other's faces; some are holding hands, their eyes restless, window-shopping; some walk side by side, stony-faced, carefully not touching. I have the sudden conviction that half these people will, in a few months, be walking with someone else now walking on the avenue one half of another couple. Eventually that arrangement will terminate as well, and each man and each woman will once again be staring out the window of a room empty of companionship. This is a population in a permanent state of intermittent attachment. Inevitably, the silent apartment lies in wait.

Who could ever have dreamed there would be so many of us floating around, those of us between thirty-five and fifty-five who live alone. Thirty years of politics in the street opened a door that became a floodgate, and we have poured through in our monumental numbers, in possession of the most educated discontent in history. Yet, we seem puzzled, most of us, about how we got here, confused and wanting relief from the condition. We roam the crowded streets, in naked expectation of the last minute reprieve. For us, human density is a requirement. Density alone provides material for the perpetual regrouping that is our necessity.

The way I see it, I said yes to this and no to that, and found myself living alone. I never *did* understand that response itself is choice. For years, mine were strongly influenced only by what I took to be a grand concern: I was on my guard against the fear of loneliness. It seemed important to me that I sort out the issues of life—work and love—without securing against the terrors of a solitary old age. Fear of loneliness, I maintained, had been responsible for so many unholy bargains made by so many women that fighting the anxiety became something of a piece of politics for me. A position I took with ease, as my understanding of the matter was primitive.

I married in my mid-twenties. My husband and I had been friends, but once married we became rapidly locked into other people's ideas of a husband and a wife. One day we were a pair of serious-minded students putting our small meals on the table together, taking turns washing up, doing the laundry. The next day I was alone in the kitchen with a cookbook while he read the paper in the living room; when he looked up it was to speculate aloud, in the direction of the kitchen, about his work, our future. I grew alarmed, and so did he. Our alarm filled the apartment and became a bane of existence. This bane held our attention to a morbid degree. We seemed continuously to be brooding on why we were not happy.

We thought of ourselves as enlightened people. The idea had been to go forward into life side by side, facing outward, at the world, but now we found that we faced only inward, each toward the ignorant other. Slowly, the relationship that was meant to serve our lives became our life. The more uncertain we grew the more we protested that love was everything. Nothing, we said, was to come between us and our love. We two would be as one. That was the norm. Deviation from the norm could only unnerve and unsettle.

This policy did not take us to the promised land, it led us further out into the desert. Neither of us, it seemed, was to be allowed an independent impulse. It became habitual for one or the other to complain regularly, "How can you say you love me and want to do *that*?" Inevitably, what either he or I had wanted to do that so outraged the other was gratify an interest that served only our own separate selves, a desire the other experienced as excluding and therefore disloyal. But the restriction went against nature: the impulse kept surfacing, like a weed pushing up through concrete.

Grieving over failed intimacy (the shock and the abnormality of it), our unhappiness seemed shameful (here we were, married and more alone than when alone). Shame isolates. The isolation was humiliating. Humiliation does not bear thinking about. We began to concentrate on not thinking.

The more troubled our attachment became the more time we spent in each other's company. We were always together. It wasn't that we enjoyed being together, not at all, it was simply that we could not bear to be apart. Together, we generated tension, but alone we each fell into an intense loneliness. The loneliness was more painful than the tension, to be avoided at any cost. Eventually, if I said I was going to the store for a container of milk my husband said he'd walk along with me. The people we knew—they were all as young as we—said, Look how devoted they are. It was marriage that taught me anxiety looks like devotion, and loneliness is the human condition most rejecting of easy analysis.

The obsession with avoiding ourselves became degrading. Our own emotions were now the enemy. A protective shell grew up around all feeling. When this shell thickened the flesh at the center shriveled. Young and healthy, I felt buried alive.

At last we parted.

I remember lying in bed that first morning staring up at the small square of bedroom ceiling. I remember the sunny silence and the bliss I felt at not having to respond to: anyone. Peace, utter peace: the shadows gone, the anxiety cleared out. What remained was open space. My presence filled the tiny apartment. I stood naked in the middle of the room. I yawned and I stretched. The *idea* of love seemed an invasion. I had thoughts to think, a craft to learn, a self to discover. Solitude was a gift. A world was waiting to welcome me if I was willing to enter it alone. I put on my clothes and walked through the door.

It was the early seventies, an exciting time, and a great many women shared the excitement. We had become converts to the woman's movement. When we met, all of us, in public places, coming together again and again for the pleasure of elaborating the insight and repeating the analysis, the world expanded into an extended companionateness of extraordinary dimension. This companionateness exhilarated and sustained. Coming home from a meeting I experienced my rooms as warm and welcoming, the orderliness and the quiet a pleasure and a relief, the conversation still buzzing in my head. There was no one in the room but me, and I was far from alone. I had brought home company, wonderful company, company that gave me back myself.

But the closeness was a function of the moment—that moment when feminism had felt revolutionary—and when the moment passed, the comradeliness passed with it. Then it was as though I knew a great many people, but none of them knew each other. The illusion of an integrated life evaporated. It was back to urban social life as I had known it before my marriage: fragmented and highly strung, marked by the tensions and withdrawals of exacerbated lives and personalities, friendships that were always in and out of phase. Without domestic companionship, it startled me to see, daily connection was by no means a given.

One day I realized I was alone, not only in the apartment but in the world. If I didn't pick up that phone and make at least one call. . . . And even when I did pick up the phone, the times without number when, no matter how many calls I made, everyone was occupied, no one was available. . . . The quiet pressed in on me. The apartment resonated with its own silence. The silence deepened. Solitude was now problematic.

Loneliness, when it came, came—then as now—like a surge of physical illness. It began with a pressure behind the eyes that forced a frown onto my face. In a matter of minutes I'd be struck down, sick and sweating, misery washing through my chest, fear radiating out in waves from the pit of my stomach. I'd lie down on the couch with an open book in my hands and wait for the seizure to pass. Sometimes, though, it would go on for days, especially in the warm and dreamy seasons of the year. I can recall a thousand mornings when I've awakened into the piercing sweetness of a summer day feeling as though my bed was anchored to a gray, unpeopled landscape, while just outside the window the world is bathed in a fluid element and all the people in it are splashing about, brilliant with color, in pairs and in groups.

So here I was, no longer alone and pleased to be alone, now alone and in pain. I did the obvious then: made those phone calls, went wherever I was invited, cultivated acquaintance-ships indiscriminately; and shortly, if I wished, I could be out every night of the week. When mere sociability became intolerable, I'd give myself a little lecture on the former joys of solitude, urging myself to spend the evening reading as I had done so frequently throughout the years of my life. Then I'd lie down on the couch, barely getting through fifty pages in three hours, reading the same sentence three times before its content was absorbed, but on the couch all the same, toughing it out.

Pain produced insight and energy but not balance or detachment. Getting through a lonely evening like a patient surmounting a fever, and praising myself for not succumbing to the worst excesses of self-pity, was surely not a sign of indomitable spirit. If that was the best I could do, I might as well get married! At those words my back stiffened. I'd be damned and gone to hell first. I saw that more was involved here than a simple matter of pleasure or pain. I had begun to have a stake in living alone.

I wrote a polemic called "Against Marriage." In this piece I argued that we marry not for the adventure of self-discovery or a shared inner life, but for emotional solace of a primitive sort. What comes with the solace is insularity, an amateurish relation to solitude, and hard questions about the inner self that go unasked for years at a time. Fear of loneliness, I said, is at the heart of the matter. To secure against a fear one must move into it, live with it, face it down. To live without love or domestic intimacy, I generously allowed, was indeed to be half alive but, I concluded, what we want now is to be real to ourselves. The myth of two-shall-become-as-one is no longer useful. Living consciously is the business of our lives. If one cannot win over loneliness, at least one can learn that it's not fatal. Such knowledge becomes a strength, an ally, a weapon.

Writing these thoughts into articles and essays became my comfort and my necessity. To write clearly on the subject, I felt, was to be renewed if not redeemed. I did not notice the rhetoric riding these pages, swelling their sentences, confining thought. I had persuaded myself that to write the problem out was to put it behind me . . . and not only me. The piece produced an uproar. I was challenged on a dozen scores, and I replied on all of them. In my own ears the replies were reasonable, but the more I explained the more entrenched I became. Before I knew it, an insight had become a theory, a theory a position, a position a dogma.

I was a born ideologue: I thrived on having a position. Now I had one: to live alone is to face down loneliness. It became a litany that in the bad times strengthened me, gave me stamina and self-control. No need to review its contents. All I had to do was keep repeating the mantra.

Years passed (that's what they did: they passed). Things remained in place. Then suddenly, without warning or consent, I was thrown back on my own dogma, and after that nothing was in place. Teaching in a southern university town, I met a woman my own age, divorced with grown children away at school. She suggested I share a house with her. I thought her a sympathetic soul and decided, after years of living alone, to chance it.

I had stumbled into a remarkably compatible arrangement. Between me and this woman there were no moods, tensions, depressions, or withdrawals. We seemed never to bore, irritate, or intrude on each other. We conducted our daily lives independently, yet were always delighted to spend an evening at home together. Conversation was an ever-deepening pleasure between us, but neither of us ever made the other feel guilty for wanting to be alone. In short, the relationship was simplicity itself, and it provided us both with the joys of civilized friendship and domestic tranquillity, a condition of life I had never known.

What took me by surprise was the relief I felt at not living alone. The relief and the gratitude. After all, what was happening here? I wasn't with a lover or even with an intimate friend. I was simply sharing a house with a compatible person. I had the pleasure of coffee in the morning and a chat in the evening with a woman I enjoyed talking with and the comfort of knowing we spent the night under the same roof. It was an absence of gross loneliness that was having an extraordinary effect on me.

And it *was* extraordinary. To begin with, I felt calm every day and all through the day—deeply calm. I realized from this calm that ordinarily I sustain, and probably have for years, a kind of low-grade anxiety that seeps daily into the nervous system. Nothing to get excited about, certainly nothing I can't handle, but it's a *feeling* I have, one I had stopped registering and would not again have been aware of if it weren't for this superb calm that now came bubbling up in me a couple of times a day.

Along with the calm, I felt smoothed out inside, as though some great blue-and-white wave had cleaned me down, washing away the grit. It was then I realized I feel gritty inside, all the time. Again, nothing to get excited about, nothing that can't be handled. Just there it was. Loneliness feels gritty.

Then the fog in my head—always a shred of it floating here or there—seemed to clear out. I found myself concentrating for hours, instead of minutes, at a time. I hadn't realized until that moment how continually my attention is being shredded, the worried granulation of inner clarity that is my constant companion.

I looked around then, at my life, and I saw that I had not learned to live alone at all. What I had learned to do was strategize; lie down until the pain passed; evade; get by. I wasn't drowning, but I wasn't swimming either. I was floating on my back, far from shore, waiting to be saved.

Looking closely at a condition that hadn't been reviewed in years, I saw that once again the thing was being named; the thing I knew and had forgotten times without number; the thing that each time I name I make more my own but each time I forget makes me lose ground. I found myself remembering the time long ago when I had first understood the thing I would always forget. It was also the day I understood why I walk, why I am a walker in the city. The memory materialized so powerfully that suddenly the day was standing before me:

I had been wandering around the apartment for hours, avoiding the desk. Couldn't think, couldn't write. My head filling up with fog, mist, cotton wool, dry ice; the fog rolling in through the window tops. The usual. The daily experience. The condition I struggle with from nine in the morning on, fighting to occupy a small clear space in my head until two or three in the afternoon when I desert the effort, feeling empty and defeated and as if I haven't heard the sound of a human voice in a thousand years.

That afternoon I had an appointment uptown, at an address three miles from my house, and on impulse I decided to walk. When I hit the street it was as though I'd emerged from a cave into the light. Everything I saw—shops, lights, cars, people— looked interesting to me. I took a deep breath and felt my lungs swell. Then I ran into someone I hadn't seen in years. The exhilaration of the unexpected encounter! My stride lengthened. I got where I was going, did what I'd gone to do, and decided to walk back. When I got home I saw that the bad feeling had washed out of me. I was purged. The walk had purged me.

I realized then how ordinary my depression was. Ordinary and predictable, ordinary and daily. Daily depression, that's all it was. I saw, as though for the first time, that daily depression eats energy. Without energy inner life evaporates; without inner life there is no animation; without animation there is no work. A life in thrall to daily depression is doomed to mediocrity.

In the same moment I saw that *this* was loneliness, the thing itself. Loneliness was the evaporation of inner life. Loneliness was me cut off from myself. Loneliness was the thing nothing out there could cure.

The depression was, I knew, rooted in a grievance that was old, older than love, older than marriage, older than friendship or politics. The grievance was my dear friend, my close friend. I had given up many others over the years, but not this one, never this one. This one, I saw, had been given the run of the house.

I knew enough to know that I would not hold on to what I was now seeing: that something in me would refuse to absorb the information. I would forget. I would not take it in. I would be overwhelmed again. Insight alone could not save me. I'd have to clear out each day anew. Walking had purged me, washed me clean, but only for that day. I understood the dailiness of the task. I was condemned to walk.

More important, I was condemned to live with what I could not take in.

We all were. Those of us who live alone; treading water; waiting for a pardon; clinging to the most educated discontent in history.

III

I walk up Columbus Avenue with new respect for life in a solitary state. I look into the avid, searching faces and I think, How well we are doing here in the brutal filthy city, those of us who stare out the window of a room empty of companionship, with the taste of grit in the morning coffee, low-grade anxiety in the evening drink. Out there, in America, our faces are withdrawn and remote, made eccentric by isolation. On Columbus Avenue collective loneliness is a stable element. It has culture-making properties.

7 on letter writing

IN 1920 WHEN MY MOTHER WAS EIGHTEEN years old she worked in the accounts department of a large wholesale bakery in Lower Manhattan. The chief bookkeeper was, like herself, a European immigrant who read books and listened to music. Mr. Levinson (an unhappily married man who lived in the Bronx) saw in my mother (a soulful young woman who lived on the Lower East Side) a kindred spirit. When they parted at the end of the working day his need for her conversation had often not run its course and he fell into the habit of writing to her late at night. These letters were remarkably varied in mood and content. They might begin reflectively at the point where the discussion had ended that day; or announce suddenly he'd been to the theater and was drenched in longing for he knew not what; or that a child was sick, the apartment in chaos, and his life a hell. The language might be poetic in tone or cynical or despairing: variations of response he allowed himself only in writing, never face to face at the bakery. Whatever the subject, whatever the mood, when Mr. Levinson sat down at midnight to write to My Dear Friend he wrote at length and at leisure. If he'd been to the theater he described the play, the acting, the crowd on Fourteenth Street; if a child was sick he confided the atmosphere in the room, the look of the patient, how the doctor had conducted himself; if he was continuing an earlier conversation he included nuance and digression freely and fully. Inevitably, he would speak of how many were his thoughts and how hungry his spirit; he'd observe the weather at the present moment, the way the street looked from the window beyond the table where he sat writing; and often he ended by telling my mother he was now going down to the corner to mail this letter so that she would read it at eight in the morning before they met an hour later at work. This last—that she'd read it in the morning—he predicted with an assurance he was entitled to: there were then five mail deliveries a day in New York.

This morning my phone rang at nine o'clock. It was my friend Laura, an academic, calling from Iowa City where she works and lives. I said, Hello, she said, Hello. I said, Everything all right? She said, Ye-e-s. I said, What is it? She launched into a familiar tale of discontent: her need for a more enlivening conversation with her husband than the one she has. The subject is territory we have traversed many times over many years, yet it remains absorbing to both of us, useful in fact. My friendship with Laura is an intimacy of more than two decades characterized by a running commentary on the dailiness of our lives and conducted almost entirely on the telephone. When we talk we each cradle the receiver, stare unseeing into the emptiness of the rooms we occupy, and concentrate on the exchange. Inevitably, these conversations are laced through with our mutual intensities—literature, politics, analysis—yet they do not wander, and within minutes it is often clear that once again we are pursuing our ongoing interest—the nature of true well-being—as though the long-distance call is a seminar in which we are both permanently enrolled. Now, this morning, as we rehearsed the well-worn arguments for and against Laura remaining in her marriage the give-and-take between us was rapid, informed, sympathetic. It supplied instant catharsis. Entertained and refreshed by the wisdom of our insights, the range of our references, the sophistication of our gossip (comparable situations provide necessary texture), we were soon persuaded that we were going forward. At the end of an hour Laura felt renewed and I felt clarified. We replaced our receivers fortified against the anxiety of the coming day.

Seventy years ago when Mr. Levinson wanted to relieve his overflowing heart he wrote a letter to my mother. This morning when the same need drove my friend Laura she picked up the telephone and called me. The result, in a sense, was also the same—connection had been made, a vital exchange extended, the courage for life restored—but surely the difference signifies. Levinson's letter was discursive, and narrative in nature. He had a subject (that is, a reason for writing) but he didn't hesitate to ramble, digress, describe everything in sight, give in restlessly to the easy pull of mood change (in the letters he sighs, he yearns, he accuses). As he writes he is placing himself in the world, alone and with the rapture of the poet. Laura's call was focused, and analytic in nature. She did not really digress, nor could she indulge herself in mood change at my expense—I was right there on the line—but as she spoke she too was placing herself: on the landscape inside her head and with the absorption of an analysand. Mr. Levinson's letter resembles the social novel of a hundred years ago and Laura's phone call a piece of twentieth-century minimalism. Each performs a stunning task of the human intelligence, comparable but not equivalent. Yet one has all but replaced the other. Why? And what does it mean?

In a recent review of the correspondence of Henry and William James, the English writer John Bayley recalled a poem of Phillip Larkin's that recreates "a world in which letters were greedily received and faithfully dispatched; in which the telephone was an expensive and barbarous mode of communication . . . and letters . . . relied on to combat the ills of daily existence." Bayley reminded us that Auden said, "To 'long for certain letters' is to be fully human, and to admit a common humanity"; and he concluded that letter writing was a noble enterprise that went uninterrupted "until our own day, when technology has all but killed off the form."

Bayley's last words stimulated an inner dialogue that raised in me the question for which I had no ready answer.

How true, I said to myself. In my youth I was a great letter writer and would have continued to be one if it wasn't for . . .

Nonsense, I answered myself. You can't blame technology for this. The question to ask is, Why didn't letter writing put up more of a fight? What is it in us that allowed the telephone such an easy takeover? Look to your own part in it. Ask yourself why *you* don't write letters anymore. Something deeper at work, I think, than "the telephone did it."

Why, indeed, do I not write letters anymore? Why, if I am honest with myself, is it tiresome to me to write a letter, an obligation I avoid as long as I can. Why do I think of letter writing as something that saps my energy and granulates my brain when, in fact, if I force myself to sit down to a letter I fall into a trance of pleasure that is undeniably restorative. So why do I fight it? Why the divided will?

Thirty-five years ago, when I was a college student, people wrote letters. The schoolteacher, the insurance agent, the social worker; the businessman who read, the lawyer who traveled; the dressmaker in evening school, the matron in community work; my unhappy mother, our expectant neighbor: all conducted an often large and varied correspondence. It was the accustomed way of ordinarily educated people to occupy the world beyond one's own small and immediate life. Entertainment was cheap and in New York, then as now, most people went regularly to movies, concerts, and plays, yet time seemed to hang about us in large open spaces. At home the phone rang only rarely and the television set was hardly ever on. The apartment was richly quiet. If you had a taste for your own thoughts it wasn't difficult to pursue them, and if you wanted to connect over them—talk, reflect, enlarge upon with a sympathetic or kindred spirit—you sat down and wrote a letter.

My friends and I were all great letter writers, that is, steady and devoted practitioners. There was always one of us out in the world: a classmate traveling in Europe or Mexico, another working in California, a third going to school in Boston. We got around, and when we did we wrote to each other. We never called, we wrote. Receiving a letter was an excitement. I'd run upstairs, kick off my shoes, fall into a comfortable chair, rip open the envelope and settle down to a good read. That was the excitement: the promise of a good read. I might not get it—my friend might not be a good writer—but no matter, the promise remained; and then I'd have the letter in my hand to read over, consult with, and refer to. This last was important because almost as soon as I'd finished reading the letter I'd start framing the sentences in my head I'd be committing to paper when, in a day or two, I sat down to write my reply.

I treasured these hours between the time I got a letter and the time I answered it. I loved ordering my thoughts, savoring the agenda. What did I want to say and in what order would I say it? How would I arrange fact and impression to let my friend know how things were with me: describe a mood, pass on information, think out loud about a book or an event, build an atmosphere on the page larger than the facts. Writing a letter was a greater pleasure than receiving one, yet a shared excitement. The sentences, when they came, seemed to issue with an unbroken fluency. I realize now that my letters, typed out on a manual typewriter, looked like Mr. Levinson's— clean, not a line rewritten or crossed out—as though we were both tapping into a collective flow of letter writing: practiceed and sure-footed.

Today, letter writing is a chore. I will not linger over what I write. In my letters I do not elaborate unnecessarily; I do not associate widely; I do not describe at length or at leisure. And still, it will take me hours to write a letter properly. I must, after all, compose it. I cannot scribble down a set of notes. I must write full sentences in full paragraphs. I must make the paragraphs agree with one another, speak to one another, cohere as a piece of writing. The expressiveness lies in the writing and that, after all, is the task of the letter: to communicate expressively. It's a decision now to write a letter whereas when I was a girl it was a way of life. It's a decision to pick up the phone as well—I must deliver on the phone too—but one I make with ease and regularity. Given the alternative between making a call and writing a letter I'd have to conclude that I prefer the call because that is what I opt for nine times out of ten. But I don't prefer it. It is simply what I do. It is what everyone does: the habitual response of the world I find myself in, that which does not require an active will.

The world I find myself in. Now there's a phrase to linger over. A phrase that furrows the brow; resonates unpleasantly in the head; even presses on the heart. What does it mean to find yourself in the world, rather than that you struggle to take your place in the world? Sounds amnesiac, somehow; anesthetized; stopped in place. Somewhere in that phrase, I believe, lies the buried history of "the telephone did it."

I remember the first time the phrase struck me. The year was 1977, the place Tel Aviv. I'd been living in the city for some months, in a flat not far from Dizengoff Street. Dizengoff was famous for its café life, and I'd been looking forward to a bit of Paris in the Middle East, but when I got there the cafés were empty. At first I didn't get it. I'd make an appointment to meet someone at a café in the evening, and I'd walk through the darkened streets thinking, Tonight it will be different. Tonight the cafés will be full. But they never were. Café life in Tel Aviv, it seemed, was over.

One night I left my flat with an Israeli journalist I'd been interviewing. This man, like many Israeli intellectuals, was famously depressed. People were surprised that he had agreed to see me. As we walked the journalist called my attention to the blue light of the television screen flickering in the darkened front rooms all around us. "Television," he said bitterly.

"A few years ago they would all have been out in the cafés, now they're home watching *Dallas.*" Television, he said, had in effect killed off café life.

It was not what the journalist said that startled me, it was the way he said it. His voice was hard and filled with resentment. He spoke as though something had been done to him. I asked him if *he* still went to the cafés. "No," he replied moodily. "What is the use? No one goes anymore." Where, then, did he and his friends gather to talk? "People don't talk anymore," he said. What do you mean, people don't talk anymore? I continued. He lived among the most urgent talkers in the world, how could he say people didn't talk anymore? "For God's sake," he cried. "The world has changed. I find myself in a world I don't recognize. What can *I* do about it? Nothing, I can do nothing; people don't talk anymore." I understood then: *he* didn't talk anymore. The cafés had done for him what he could not do for himself. What he would not do for himself. Now that the cafés were emptying out, people didn't talk anymore.

I never forgot the inertness beneath the anger in the journalist's voice: the hard dull passivity in it. The world had let him down. He had expected it to be one way, and it was turning out another. He had *done* the best he could. No one could say he hadn't been willing to talk. When the cafés were there he'd gone to them. Now that he found himself in a world without cafés . . . well, what could you expect?

At the time I didn't know I was going to remember the

sound of this voice, and the burden of its message, for years to come, but now that I am thinking about all the letters I don't write I see that I am gazing into the memory of that exchange.

I was home reading. A friend called to tell me of the shootings of the Lubavitcher students on the Brooklyn Bridge. At eleven o'clock I turned on the television set to get a full report. There were three stories that evening—the shootings, an airplane's nosedive at La Guardia Airport, and I've forgotten the third—interspersed among commercials, rising theme music, broadcasters gossiping among themselves, ten or fifteen rapid-talking people sticking a microphone into the face of half a hundred other people. When I turned off the set I went back to my book but I had become restless. I couldn't concentrate, couldn't think. The sound of television noise lingered in my head. It began to mingle with the street noise I had managed to block out for an hour or two. At this point my phone rang. I didn't answer it, but my answering machine did. The room was filled now with the remembered din of the television set, the endless scream of the street below my windows, the clacking noise coming from my desk. I lay on the couch, spacing out with the book in my hands. When, at last, I was able to hypnotize myself back into an illusioned quiet the silence came as a relief. That was it: relief. I realized then that never again in my life would the quiet that surrounds me be as rich and animated as it had been in my childhood: when everyone wrote letters. I stared at the ceiling, and I resented the world as it is. Resentment flared into anger; anger sank into depression; depression gave way to lethargy. I read no more that night.

A few days later I had to deliver a piece of information to a friend of mine who lives in Soho, one zip code away from my apartment. I reached for the phone, then stopped, my hand hovering over the receiver. I did not, at that moment, want to talk to my friend. I did not want to hear her voice, I did not want to hear my own. Yet, I wanted to speak to her. Suddenly, I wanted to write a letter. I wanted to tell my friend on paper how the information had come into my hands, what I had thought when I'd received it, what I was thinking now. I wanted to describe the light in my room as I was writing, the air as it had felt when I came home, an exchange I had just had in the elevator. I wanted, in short, to narrate not to transmit; to enlarge upon the moment; impose shape; achieve form. It would be a different piece of information my friend would then receive, coming through the mail rather than over the phone, the kind of information one might get from a poem not a memo: a piece of intimacy I wanted to offer her, to extend myself.

No sooner did I sit down at the computer than the impulse began to fragment. It had been a long day. I was tired. I was going out again in two hours. Did I have enough time to write this? I consulted the groove in my brain for letter-writing sentences. It felt stiff and narrow. So long since I'd written a letter! Maybe tomorrow morning. Then I remembered that my friend needed the information within two days. If I wrote, she might have my letter day after tomorrow, then again she might have it in a week. I could not rely on mail delivery. What the hell, I thought, take a chance. I turned on the computer. God, I was tired! I turned off the machine and picked up the phone.

"Darling!" my friend said. Therapeutic vibrancy flowed across the wire. I told her what she needed to know. Then I told her that I had wanted to write, not call. "Really!" she laughed and sympathized instantly with my predicament; she had often been in it herself. We discussed the psychology of the matter in quick, flashing sentence fragments. I began to feel enlivened and refreshed as we spoke, but ten minutes later I hung up as tired as before I'd made the call. More than tired. Defeated, somehow. The link between the light, the air, the information, and the elevator encounter was lost to me: I would never make it now. Something important seemed trapped in that loss.

I sat at my desk staring at the telephone. I didn't hate the phone, or the conversation I had just had on it, but it was hateful to me that I had succumbed to the dictates of the phone call. It was not at all what had been needed or wanted. At that moment life seemed smaller.

Okay, I began to argue with myself. So you spoke over the phone instead of on paper. It's *hard* to organize written response, it *always* means making an extra effort. But you *do* make the connection. You're *always* calling. For God's sake, isn't that enough?

No, I answered myself. It's not enough. To transmit is one thing, to narrate another—comparable but not interchangeable. Choosing between them is like choosing between work and love: either way, it's half a life. I saw then what was at stake in the matter of the letter and the phone call.

The telephone conversation is, by its very nature, reactive not reflective. Immediacy is its prime virtue. The immediacy delivers quick company, instant stimulation; the stimulation is cathartic; catharsis pushes back anxiety; into open space flows the kind of thought generated by electric return. The letter, written in absorbed solitude, is an act of faith; it assumes the presence of humanity; world and self are generated from within; loneliness is courted not feared. To write a letter is to be alone with my thoughts in the conjured presence of another person. I keep myself imaginative company. I occupy the empty room. I alone infuse the silence. All things Mr. Levinson did when he sat down at midnight seventy years ago to write to my mother.

Levinson never knew the pleasures of unguarded speech, that extraordinary gift of the therapeutic culture. Alone at midnight with pen, ink, and paper he achieved only the joy of the shaped sentence. That joy took him where spoken conversation could not, made him press into places in himself he otherwise never went. The letters are a record of his longing to make sense of things, penetrate his own chaos, figure out what he feels from what he is writing. A different kind of inner pursuit: a journey into unmapped space. Transmission is a series of connecting signals sent out across the exploratory surface. Narration is a road cut in the wilderness. Both are wanted in a life. Each alone is an insufficiency of experience. One replaces the other only at great cost, but we seem always to be living in a world that tells us both are uneconomical, one or the other will do.

When café life thrives talk is a shared limberness of the mind that improves the appetite for conversation: an adequate sentence maker is then made good, a good one excellent, an excellent one extraordinary. When the whole world is writing letters it's easy to tap into the quiet within, tell the story of an hour, keep alive the narrating inner life. To be alone in the presence of one's own thought then is not a value, only a common practice. It's when the cafés empty out and mail delivery is uncertain that the struggle to stay human becomes an act of deliberation.

I had wanted to risk the mail, but I hadn't wanted it enough. It hurt me to lose the narrative impulse, but I could live with the pain. Because I could live with it I am living with it. Because I'm living with it I occupy a world I find myself in. Me and the Israeli journalist.

In 1937 Edmund Wilson wrote to Louise Bogan, urging her to recover from nervous collapse by getting back to work. "We have to take life—society and human relations—more or less as we find them," Wilson wrote. "The only thing that we can really make is our work. And deliberate work of the mind, imagination and hand, done, as Nietzsche said, 'notwithstanding,' in the long run remakes the world." Conversely, work that is *not* done—deliberateness avoided—is also world-making. Every time the urge to write a letter dies stillborn in me I am making the world I rail against. I set the narrative impulse adrift. I let the noise prevail.

Letter writing is not the noble enterprise. Remaining fully expressive is the noble enterprise.

LIBRARY OF CONGRESS CATALOGING-IN-PUBLICATION DATA

Gornick, Vivian.
    Approaching eye level / Vivian Gornick.
      p. cm.
    ISBN 0-8070-7090-4 (cloth)
    ISBN 0-8070-7091-2 (paper)
    1. Gornick, Vivian. 2. Women—New York (State)—New York
—Biography. 3. Women authors—New York (State)—New York
—Biography.   I. Title.
HQ1439.N6G67 1996
305.4'09747—dc20   96-12094